Policy Environment and Regulatory Reforms for Private and Foreign Investment in Developing Countries: A Case of the Indian Power Sector

Anoop Singh

Visiting Researcher
ADB Institute, Tokyo

Associate Professor
Department of Industrial and Management Engineering
Indian Institute of Technology Kanpur

Amani International Publishers

Dr. Anoop Singh
Associate Professor
Department of Industrial and Management Engineering
Indian Institute of Technology Kanpur
E-mail: anoops@iitk.ac.in

Bibliographic information published by the Deutsche Nationalbibliothek

The Deutsche Nationalbibliothek lists this publication in the Deutsche Nationalbibliografie; detailed bibliographic data are available in the Internet at http://dnb.d-nb.de

Manufactured in Germany

E-Mail: service@amani-publishers.com
http://www.amani-publishers.com

ISBN: 978-3-938054-01-7
eISBN: 978-3-938054-28-4

Policy Environment and Regulatory Reforms for Private and Foreign Investment in Developing Countries: A Case of the Indian Power Sector

To Pushpinder, Manveer and Taranveer

Table of Content

List of Tables

List of Figures

List of Appendices

Preface

Electricity, one of the key infrastructure sectors, plays a very important role in socio-economic development of a country. Developing countries with significant gap in the provision of electricity have attempted to provide a conducive environment for investment in the power sector. Initiatives towards the same are evident in terms of opening up the sector for private and foreign investment, setting up of independent regulatory institutions and bringing regulatory and policy changes to enhance competition in the sector. However, scope, pace and sequence of such reforms varies across countries.

This book provides a detailed overview of the reform process in the electricity sector in India since the early 1990s, highlighting the key policy changes that have led to opening up the sector for investment and competition in generation, transmission and the distribution segments. This book also provides an insight into in the reform process, through a comparative assessment, adopted in key developing economies including Argentina, Brazil, China (PRC), India, Mexico and Thailand. While the book does not attempt a comprehensive analysis of the way process of power reform has influenced private investment in the power sector in developing countries. This book would be useful for research scholars, advanced graduate students in economics, multi-lateral institutions, policy makers and regulators in India as well as other developing countries, who are embarking on a path to reform the power sector. The inferences derived from the research results presented here should help policy makers, development intuitions as well as regulatory institutions in choosing an appropriate path to reform as per the country specific conditions and help attract greater private investment in the sector.

The research work presented here was initiated during the author's stay at the Asian Development Bank Institute (ADBI), Tokyo under a Visiting Researcher Fellowship programme from July – Dec. 2005. The research work was further updated and extended in scope, and was completed during the first half of 2007. The author expresses sincere thanks to the Asian Development Bank Institute, Tokyo for the award of the fellowship and support to the research work. The author would like to thank all the researchers and staff for their kind help during my stay at ADBI. Special thanks are due to Dr. Peter McCawley (Dean, ADBI) and Dr. John Weiss (Director of Research, ADBI), who provided useful inputs for the research through its various stages. The staff of the ADBI has been very kind and helpful, and provided necessary support during our stay at Tokyo. The author would also like to place on record the cooperation from other researchers at ADBI, and the researchers and fellows visiting ADBI during the same period. The authors also benefited from discussions with personnel at other related agencies in Japan especially the Institute of Energy Economics, Japan (IEEJ) and the Tokyo Electric Power Company (TEPCO). Thanks are also due for the institutional support from Indian Institute of Technology Kanpur for extending necessary cooperation to accomplish my visit to ADBI, Tokyo. The author would like to than the Center for Development of Technical Education of IIT Kanpur for necessary financial support to complete the manuscript.

Finally, I thank my wife, Pushpinder, and son, Manveer, who accompanied me during my visit to Tokyo, and provided necessary personal support and encouragement. I am joined with my family, to thank the people of Japan for their hospitality to make our stay there memorable and enjoyable one.

Anoop Singh

1

Introduction

Long-run economic growth is influenced by the availability of infrastructure services including electricity (CANNING & PEDRONI, 2004; CALDERÓN & SERVÉN, 2004)). Infrastructure is also a key component of the investment environment, in general (WORLD BANK, 2005a). It also contributes to poverty reduction and helps in bridging the income gap (ADB *et al.*, 2005). A survey of the literature on the influence of infrastructure on economic growth also reveals that infrastructure is most critical in the case of low-income and developing economies (Estache, 2004). Future growth profile of emerging economies including Brazil, Russia, India and the People's Republic of China (PRC) would be influenced by availability of various infrastructure services including electricity.

The scale of investment required in infrastructure sectors far exceeds the existing levels. Annual investment requirement for the infrastructure sector in the developing countries, between 2005 and 2010, is pegged at USD 464.79 billion including 30% (USD 139.44 billion) for electricity generation (FAY & YEPES, 2003). IEA (2003a) projects the cumulative power sector investment between 2000 and 2030 to top USD 9.84 trillion, more than half of this (USD 5.1 trillion) to be required in developing countries.

Infrastructure investment with private participation in developing countries in 2004 is estimated to be USD 64.1 billion after reaching a peak of USD 114.1 billion in 1997. Of this, investment in the electricity sector in 2004 is estimated to be only USD 12.1 billion, against a peak of USD 43.3 billion in 1997 (IZAGUIRRE, 2005). The inability of the global capital markets to meet the investment requirements in the infrastructure sector in developing countries and the recent decline in flow of private finance is attributed to the recent macroeconomic shocks, ongoing transformations in the global electricity and telecommunications industries, the weakness of the local capital markets in most developing countries, and unfinished reforms (WORLD BANK, 2004). Financial crises in the East Asian countries (1997), then in Brazil (1999) and Argentina (2001) led to steep devaluations of local currencies. Further, unfavourable conditions in the international capital market reduced the ability of the investors to raise capital for new investments. These conditions in developing countries along with previous experience of investors' in developing countries have been identified as the main reasons for the decline in foreign investors' interest in the power sector in these countries (LAMECH & SAEED, 2003). This highlights the crucial influence of macroeconomic stability, especially in influencing foreign investment. In addition to macroeconomic stability, market access, market design, and stable and effective legal and regulatory frameworks are also essential for securing foreign capital for energy projects (IEA, 2003b).

The Indian economy is poised for higher economic growth in the years to come. This will require large investment in the infrastructure sectors including the power sector. The National Electricity Plan of India aims also to provide access to electricity to all households by 2010 and to meet all shortages by 2012. This will require an investment of Rs.9000 billion (approximately USD 200 billion) at 2002-03 prices to finance generation, transmission, sub-transmission, distribution and rural electrification projects (GOI, 2005a). Against the backdrop of a peak investment of USD 114.1 billion (in 1997) in all infrastructure sectors of the developing countries, the investment requirement of the Indian power sector alone pose a serious challenge.

During the 1990s, up to 70% of infrastructure funding came from the public sector, followed by the private sector (20–25%) and official development assistance (5–10%) (DFID, 2002). Increasingly, governments are facing the need to meet competing budgeting requirement from other social sectors such as health and primary education. Need for enhanced fiscal discipline and macroeconomic stability also places a limit on borrowing capacity of the governments. Given the limited fiscal space for budgetary support for such investments, greater private sector participation is inevitable. Inefficiency, administrative bottlenecks and poor and inadequate infrastructure facilities, in particular continued shortage of electricity in developing countries under public ownership has necessitated enhanced private participation in the sector.

Designing an effective policy framework and setting up independent regulatory institutions is crucial for attracting not only private domestic but also foreign investment (SADER, 1999). This is essential for the mitigation and appropriate allocation of risks, thereby improving the bankability of power projects in the project finance market. From a literature survey of electricity sector and Latin American concession contracts, STERN & CUBBIN (2005) also find evidence for the effectiveness of regulatory agencies in promoting investment and preventing serious problems related to concession contract. From a detailed analysis of infrastructure concession projects in Latin American countries, SIRTAINE *et al.* (2005) observe that effective regulation is a package deal. The lack of a few ingredients can significantly influence the ability of investors to expect returns that exceed their cost of capital. For example, a regulatory framework founded on strong legal foundations but which lacks financial resources for the regulator, is unlikely to be very effective.

Private investors respond to risk return tradeoffs. The policy environment and regulatory framework contribute significantly to the investment environment especially in the power sector. Power sector reforms have been initiated across a number of countries with the aim of creating an enabling environment for private investment thereby helping to bridge the gap in public investment. Chile began this exercise in the late 1980s. Persistent power shortages, inadequate public investment and the economic crisis faced by India in the early 1990s led to the opening up of the power sector to private investment and major policy initiatives were undertaken to encourage private and foreign investment. The investment climate was further strengthened through gradual restructuring of the state electricity boards (SEBs) and initiation of regulatory reforms at the federal and state level. More recently, enactment of the Electricity Act 2003 includes enabling provisions for enhancing competition in the sector and to improve the environment for private participation. The abolition of the single buyer model and phased access to consumers has unlocked substantial potential for private investment in the sector. The poor state of state owned distribution utilities, a weak link in the supply chain of electricity, undermines the process of reforms and seems to have hampered private interest in the sector.

The globalisation and economic reforms have led to rise in Foreign Direct Investment (FDI) in developing countries. The traditional literature emphasises the economic advantages of FDI in developing countries (DUNNING, 1993; MORAN, 1999). The role of governance has gathered importance. The more recent literature also highlights the role of institutions and governance (KIRKPATRICK *et al.*, 2004; GLOBERMAN & SHAPIRO, 2002). KIRKPATRICK *et al.* (2004) examine the relationship between the quality of the regulatory framework and foreign direct investment in infrastructure. In another study, using data on 155 developed and developing countries between 1995 and 1997, GLOBERMAN and SHAPIRO (2002) conclude that governance infrastructure is an important determinant of both inward as well as outward FDI. A strong governance infrastructure not only attracts capital, but also creates an environment under which domestic multinational corporations emerge and invest abroad. Further, the authors find that investments in governance infrastructure are subject to diminishing returns. Hence, their ability to promote FDI is more evident for smaller and developing economies.

The main objective of this report is to provide an overview of the evolving policy environment and regulatory framework for private and foreign investment in the Indian power sector. Given that the international capital flows do not happen in vacuum, but are influenced by relative risk/return trade-off in various legal boundaries, the report provides a comparative analysis of the policy and regulatory framework in the Indian power sector with those in some of the Asian and Latin American countries. These include Argentina, Brazil, Mexico, PRC and Thailand. This is expected to help identify the areas for policy action in the Indian context and to help design policy and regulatory reform in other developing countries, especially in the Asian region.

The following section discusses the investment requirement for infrastructure sector more particularly the power sector in developing countries. Section 3 provides a statistical review of historical profile of private investment in the power sector in developing countries. Section 4 presents a brief review of the Indian power sector. The policy and regulatory developments since the early 1990s especially those with special reference to private and foreign investment are elaborated in Section Five. An analysis of the existing policy and regulatory framework leads us to present, in Section 6, the existing framework for private investment in various segments of the Indian power sector - generation, transmission, distribution and trading. Section 7 presents the status of private and foreign investment in the Indian power sector. Section 8 reviews the literature on factors influencing private investment in the power sector in developing countries. This also includes a discussion on previous work investigating the role of policy environment and regulatory reforms. A comparative analysis of the policy and regulatory environment in the power sector across the five identified nations and India is presented in section nine. One of the important components of the policy and regulatory framework is to determine or to influence the rate of return for investors. Section ten provides an assessment of the rate of return framework in some of the identified countries by reviewing the related literature. The mode of private participation varies across the identified countries. This is taken up for discussion in section 11. The role of multilateral development institutions and the project distress issues are discussed in sections 12 and 13 respectively. While the role of foreign capital is expected to increase, role of domestic capital would play a dominant role. This is discussed in section fourteen. Section 15 brings out the key recommendations related to policy and regulatory environment for encouraging private and foreign investment in India. Finally, Section sixteen concludes the report by summarising the key findings and charting out a scope for further research in the area.

2

Power Sector Investment in Developing Countries: Requirements and Prospects

Economic growth depends significantly on the supply of energy, including electricity. This is more so in the case of under-developed and developing countries, which have an elastic GDP-to-energy relationship. More than half of the investment requirement in the electricity sector over the next three decades is required in developing countries (Table 1). This is higher than the investment requirement in OECD countries. Roughly half of the investment demand from developing countries will be accounted for by PRC and India.

Between 1992 and 2003, infrastructure investment in developing countries was estimated to be USD 622 billion - an average of USD 52 billion a year and representing 3.8% of total gross domestic investment in the developing world. Approximately two-thirds of this investment was in East Asian and Latin American countries. South Asian countries have lagged behind in this aspect (World Bank, 2005b). Annual investment requirement for new infrastructure stock and for maintenance of existing infrastructure stock in developing countries, between 2005 and 2010, is estimated to be USD 233.14 billion and USD 231.65 billion respectively. Electricity generation alone would account for over USD74 billion and around USD64 billion respectively for new capital investment and maintenance of existing facilities (Fay & Yepes, 2003). Projections by IEA (2003a) (USD 170 billion per year for the electricity sector in developing countries) over a longer horizon (till 2030) present even a more daunting task (Table 1). The gap between investment requirement and the historical investment profile highlights the presence of a larger financial gap for the sector.

The demand for investment in the electricity sector in the world stands at an astonishing USD 9.8 trillion between 2000 and 2030, including about 40 % of this for power generation alone. The Indian power sector would require an investment of USD665 billion during the same period (IEA, 2003a). It should also be noted that power sector investment in PRC is estimated to be over 2% of the GDP in the year 2000.

Table 1
Investment Outlook for Electricity Sector (USD billion)

	2001-10	2011-20	2021-30	2001-30
		World		
Generation	926	1422	1731	4080
Refurbishment	145	152	142	439
Transmission	439	548	581	1568
Distribution	1052	1274	1429	3755
Total	2562	3396	3883	9842
		OECD Countries		
Generation	390	595	734	1719
Refurbishment	98	90	71	260
Transmission	188	209	172	569
Distribution	520	507	461	1488
Total	1196	1401	1438	4036
		Developing Countries		
Generation	501	704	859	2064
Refurbishment	35	46	57	138
Transmission	230	307	382	918
Distribution	452	664	871	1987
Total	1218	1721	2169	5107
		PRC		
Generation	199	285	311	795
Refurbishment	13	17	20	50
Transmission	90	119	136	345
Distribution	175	254	294	723
Total	477	675	761	1913
		India		
Generation	69	83	116	268
Refurbishment	4	5	6	15
Transmission	29	39	51	119
Distribution	44	85	134	262
Total	146	212	307	664

Source: IEA (2003a)

Investment in the power sector in developing countries has slowed down and is far less than the need of the sector[1]. The power sector in developing countries needs to compete with other infrastructure sectors, which also require substantial investment. Developing countries also have to compete with significant investment demand in OECD countries. In attracting investment, developing countries need to address concerns associated with additional risks in these countries. The Indian power sector has not been able to attract substantial private investment, in proportion to its requirements, due to its inadequate legal and commercial framework, and delays in obtaining regulatory approvals (IEA, 2003a). There is also increasing competition among developing countries for attracting FDI in the power sector. The existence of this multitude of competing investment destinations further strengthens the argument for improving the investment climate in the country.

Faced with subdued interest by the private sector, the challenges for the host countries wishing to attract private investment are mounting. In a survey of 65 private investors in the power sector, LAMECH and SAEED (2003) find that over half of investors were either hoping to retreat from these markets or were less interested than before in pursuing new opportunities. High-yield investment opportunities and improved corporate profitability in the developed world would sharpen competition for investment funds destined for developing countries (WORLD BANK, 2005b).

Table 2
Number of Countries Adopting Key Reforms in the Power Sector

	Region (number of countries)					
Key Step	AFR (48)	EAP (9)	ECA (27)	LAC (18)	MNA (8)	SA (5)
Corporate	15 (31%)	4 (44%)	17 (63%)	11 (61%)	2 (25%)	2 (40%)
Law	7 (15%)	3 (33%)	11 (41%)	14 (78%)	1 (13%)	2 (40%)
Regulator	4 (8%)	1 (11%)	11 (41%)	15 (83%)	0 (0%)	2 (40%)
IPPs	9 (19%)	7 (78%)	9 (33%)	15 (83%)	1 (13%)	5 (100%)
Restructuring	4 (8%)	4 (44%)	14 (52%)	13 (72%)	3 (38%)	2 (40%)
Generation privatization	2 (4%)	2 (22%)	10 (37%)	7 (39%)	1 (13%)	2 (40%)
Distribution privatization	2 (4%)	1 (11%)	8 (30%)	8 (44%)	1 (13%)	1 (20%)
Reform indicator	0.88	2.44	2.7	4.28	1	3
Reform indicator (%)	15%	41%	45%	71%	17%	50%

Source: UNDP/World Bank (1999)

Note: AFR = Africa: EAP = East Asia and Pacific: ECA = Europe and Central Asia: LAC = Latin America and the Caribbean: MNA = Middle East and North Africa: SA = South Asia.

[1] This is further discussed in the next section.

A number of developing countries have embraced reforms of the power sector and have undertaken policy initiatives to improve the investment climate for the private sector. UNDP/World Bank (1999) find that countries in the Latin America and the Caribbean, and the South Asian regions were at the forefront of such initiatives (Table 2).

These reforms have yielded results and the flow of private capital to the power sector in developing countries was initially promising during the last decade, before slow down primarily due to economic crises in the East Asia and Latin America. In the following section, we discuss the spatial as well as temporal profile of private investment in the power sector in developing countries.

3

Private Participation in the Power Sector in Developing Countries

The 1990s witnessed active private investment in the power sector in developing countries. As a result of reforms in the sector, and the unshackling of the sector from public ownership and investment, annual private investment reached a peak of USD 43.3 billion in 1997 (Fig. 1). The impressive growth of private investment in the 1990s was also propelled by increasing demand, restrictions on concessionary loans by multilateral lending institutions and, seeking fresh investment opportunities bring sought by the investors in the US and Europe, who were facing liquidity with low returns (WOODHOUSE, 2005a). Latin American and East Asian countries were prime destination for the investment (Fig. 2).

The pattern of private investment in Latin America was dominated by divestiture of government owned assets[2]. Significant political resistance to privatisation South Asia limited divestiture of government owned utilities. Most of the private investment in the region was utilised for setting up green field power projects (Fig. 2). This difference stems from differences in the approach to power sector reform followed in some of the countries in the two regions. The reforms of the power sector in India and other countries in the South Asian region emphasised private investment in generation, and created little space for private investors in the politically sensitive distribution segment, which is owned by respective state governments. The reform strategy followed by some of Latin American countries realised the benefit of distribution reforms coupled with privatisation. The strategy seems to have paid off well in attracting private investment in the sector.

[2] For e.g., between April 1992 and June 1995, over 25 state-operated power companies were privatized. All private investment in Mexico is on account of divestiture of government owned assets.

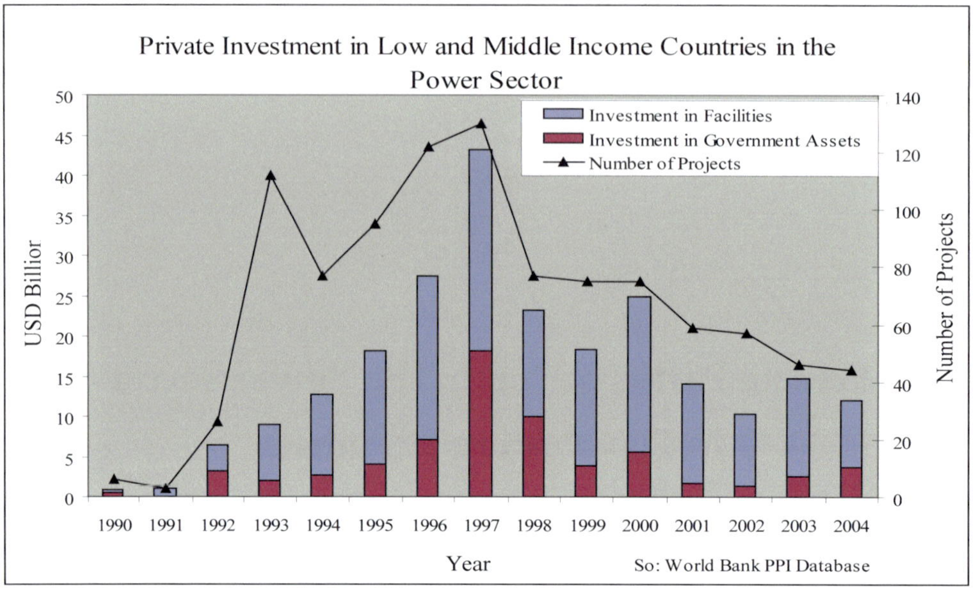

Fig. 1 Private Investment in Low- and Middle-Income Countries in the Power Sector

The East Asian financial crisis in 1997 put a number of IPPs at risk, primarily in Indonesia. The private investment in the power sector in the East Asian region dropped significantly from USD 12.7 billion in 1997 to USD 5.2 billion in 1998. In the aftermath of the crisis, the governments of Thailand and the Philippines came to the rescue of troubled greenfield power projects (Woo, 2005a; Woodhouse, 2005b). The East Asian crisis did not significantly dampen the investors' sentiments in South Asia, where private investment grew from USD1.5 billion in 1997 to over USD 3.0 billion in 2000, though it is possible that it would have reached higher levels in the absence of the crisis (Fig. 3). Crow (2001) also notes that following the East Asian crisis in the late 1990s, non-insurable economic *force majeure* conditions[3] have significantly influenced FDI in the power sector in developing countries, and remain a key concern for investors. The financial crisis in Argentina, an erstwhile abode for private investors, further dampened investors' interest in the sector. Subsequently, private investment in the power sector in the South Asian region dropped to USD 860 million in 2001 and to USD 415 million in 2003. The fading memories of the earlier crises and the continuity of the reform process led to an increase in private investment, which rose up to USD 3.5 billion in 2004. The number of projects also witnessed a similar trend (Fig. 4).

[3] These include exchange rate depreciation, decline in GDP growth and unpredictable structural change.

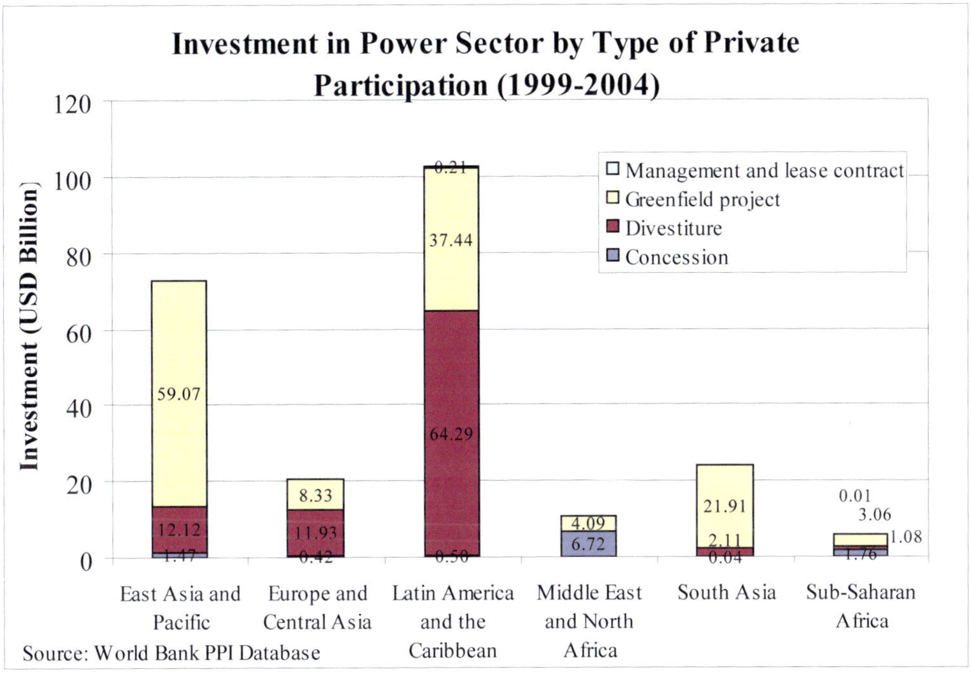

Fig. 2 Investment in Power Sector by Type of Private Participation

The drop in private participation in Latin American countries after 1997 can also be attributed to the accomplishment of significant privatisation of distribution companies in some of the countries of the region. This also hints at the potential for private investment in the South Asian region where the privatisation of distribution companies has failed to make progress due to political hurdles, but where the potential for future progress cannot be ruled out. Poor access to electricity in the South Asian region (43%) as compared to Latin America (89%) and East Asia (88%) also suggests greater investment need and potential for private participation (World Bank, 2005c).

Based on the expectation of significant investment from the private sector, multilateral institutions such as the World Bank reduced their infrastructure lending in the nineties. The World Bank's lending to the infrastructure sector dropped from USD 9.5 billion in 1993 to USD 5.5 billion in 2002 (World Bank, 2003). However, declining private participation in the infrastructure sector due to a number of economic crises that hit countries in East Asia and Latin America, subsequently prompted the Bank to increase lending for the sector. By the year 2005, the Bank's infrastructure lending[4] rose to USD 7.4 billion, represent-

[4] With increased emphasis on urban development.

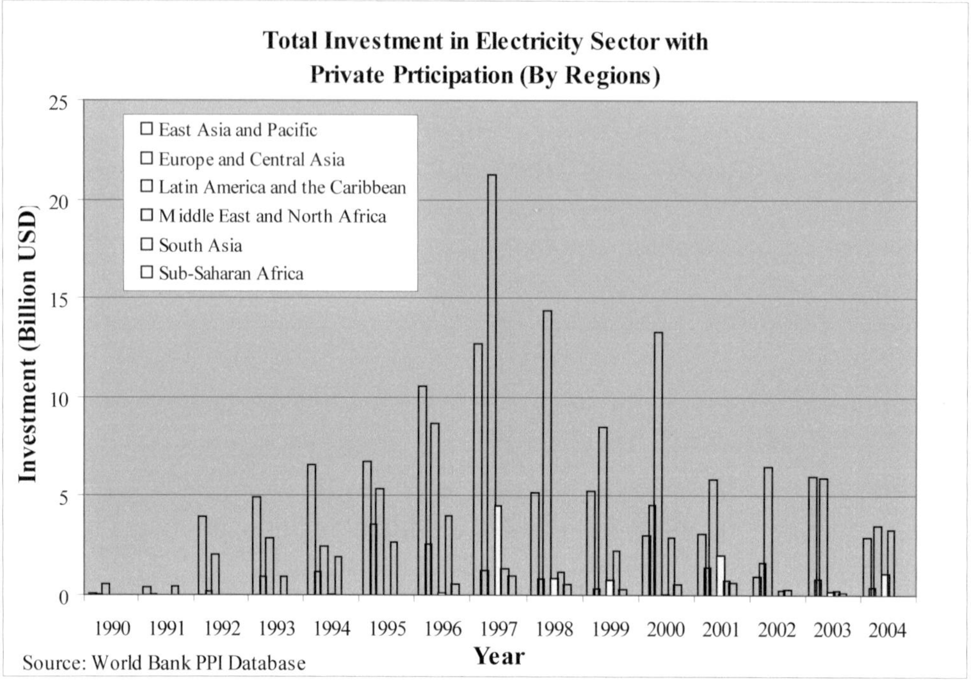

Fig. 3 Private Investment in the Power Sector: A Regional Landscape

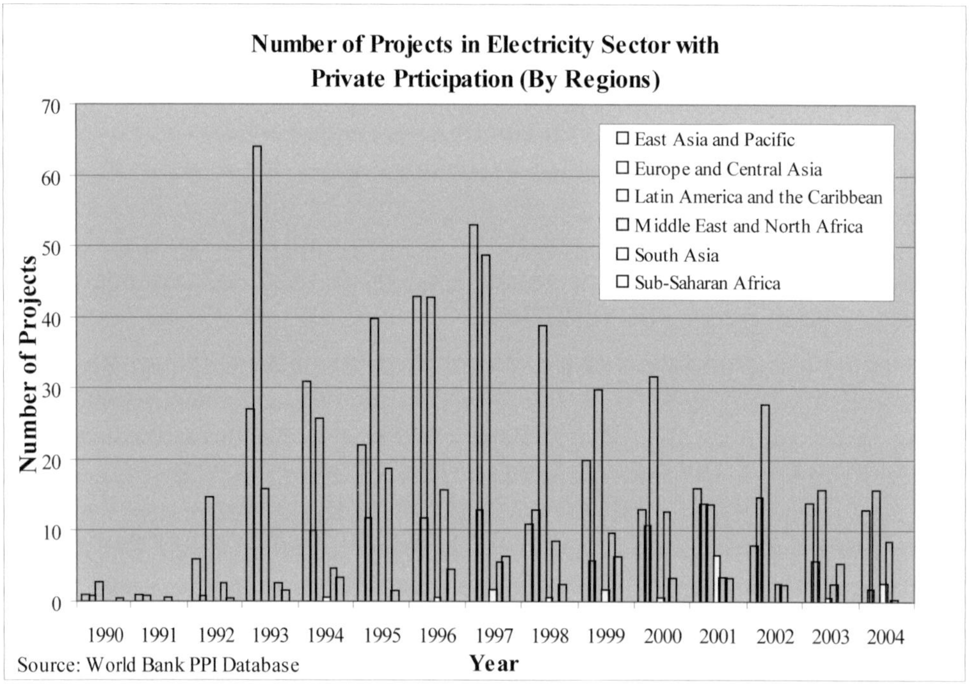

Fig. 4 Number of New Private Projects in the Power Sector: A Regional Landscape

ing 33% of its total portfolio (WORLD BANK, 2005c). However, composition of the Bank's portfolio does not present a rosy picture as allocation for Energy and Mining (including the power sector) dropped from 40.7% in year 2002 to 25.3% in 2005. Against this, the commitment of International Finance Corporation (IFC) increased marginally from USD 722 million in 2002 to USD 800 million in 2005. In terms of investment guarantees, which are often sought by private investors, the share of the infrastructure sector in MIGA's portfolio grew from 29% in 2001 to 38% in 2005 (WORLD BANK, 2005c).

The scale of private sector investment in the power sector in Latin American region can perhaps be explained by reform steps implemented by a number of countries in the region (Refer to Section 2, Table 2). The South Asian region fared second best in this context, but fared poorly in terms of restructuring and the privatisation of the distribution segment. Does reforming the last node of the electricity supply chain hold the key to attracting private investment? As discussed later, this may be the case.

Some of the developing countries, including India, are making progress in their efforts to induce private investment in the power sector. However, improving growth prospects in domestic markets may encourage international project promoters to look inward to their own domestic markets unless lucrative returns are forthcoming under an appropriate investment climate. As the shadow of the East Asian crisis fades is fading, India is facing increasing policy competition to remain an attractive destination for attracting private and foreign investment. The next two sections present an overview of the Indian power sector followed by a discussion on the policy and regulatory reforms implemented since the early 1990s.

4

The Indian Power Sector: An Overview

Decades of economic planning in India following independence placed significant emphasis on the development of the power sector. Electricity generation capacity with utilities in India has grown from 1713 MW as on Dec. 1950 to over 124,287 MW by March 2006 (CEA, 2006a). However, per capita electricity consumption remains much lower than the world average and even lower than some of the developing Asian economies (Table 3).

Table 3
Per Capital Electricity Consumption (2003)

S. No.	Country	Per Capital Electricity Consumption (kWh)
1.	Argentina	2185
2.	Brazil	1883
3.	PRC	1379
4.	India (2004-05)	613
5.	Japan	7818
6.	Mexico	1801
7.	Thailand	1752
8.	USA	13078
9.	World	2456

Source: World Bank (2006) and CEA (2006a)

Investment in the sector has not been able to improve access and keep pace with the country's growing demand for electricity (SINGH, 2006). As on March 2005, the official statistics state that 85% of India's 587,000 villages have been electrified. However, the recent population census (2001) reveals that 44.2% of the households do not have access to electricity. Consumers, who are connected to the grid, also face severe power shortages. The energy shortage was recorded to be 7.4% (7.1%) in 2004-05 (2003-04). The peak shortage was estimated to be 10.5% (11.2%) in 2004-05 (2003-04). The last decade of the previous century witnessed some of the worst power supply situations yet. Peaking shortages reached 20.49% in 1992-93 and energy shortages reached 11.7% in 1996-97 (CEA, 2005a, 2006a). Power shortages are real and are hurting the competitiveness of the economy. Due to the lack of a reliable grid supply, industrial units are installing generators. While about 21% of Chinese firms and 17% of Brazilian firms own electricity generators, 61% of the Indian firms have generators installed to cope with power shortages. Real cost of power in India is 39% higher than that in the PRC (WB/IFC, 2004).

The Sixteenth Electric Power Survey projects a capacity requirement of about 100,000 MW for the period 2002-12 (CEA, 2001). Apart from generation capacity addition and associated network strengthening, additional investment is required to extend the transmission and distribution network to meet the requirement of the unserved population. A new rural electrification scheme, Rajiv Gandhi Grameen Vidyutikaran Yojana, was introduced in April 2005. It targets to electrify all villages and provide access to all households within five years. The Indian power sector requires an investment of Rs.9000 billion (approximately USD 200 billion) at 2002-03 prices to finance generation, transmission, sub-transmission, distribution and rural electrification projects (GOI, 2005a). IEA (2003a) estimates the total investment requirement in the Indian power sector (for the period 2000–30) – including generation, refurbishment, transmission and distribution – to be USD665 billion. Such requirements reflect the foreseeable economic growth in the years to come.

The poor financial status and operational efficiency of SEBs/state utilities is imposing a heavy burden on the economic resources of the respective state governments. On the financial side, the lack of expenditure prudence and skewed tariff structure has led to a deterioration of the financial health of state utilities[5]. The gap between the average cost of supply and average tariff increased from 50 paise/kWh in 1996-97 to 110 paise/kWh in 2001-02. The number of subsidized categories, assisted by the growing network and rural electrification drive, increased. However, an increasing number of consumers, including industrial and commercial consumers have acquired captive power generation capacities that provide better economy, quality and reliability. Poor operational and technical

[5] For further discussion on some of the key concerns in the Indian power sector, see Singh (2006).

efficiency, along with the above factors, has resulted in ballooning financial losses in the sector. The commercial losses of SEBs (before subsidy) during 2001-02 were estimated to be Rs. 331.77 billion as compared to Rs. 113.05 billion during 1996-97. After including the subsidy payable by state governments, the above figures are Rs. 248.37 billion and Rs.46.74 billion, respectively.

The average consumer tariff for state utilities during 2004-05 (2003-04) is estimated to be 359.39 paise (361.00 paise). After including electricity departments in the Union Territories, this is estimated to be 276.54 paise (274.29 paise). The gap between average cost of supply and average tariff declined from 114.83 paise/kWh in 2000-01 to 82.85 paise/kWh in 2004-05 (RE) 86.71 (provisional). The loss on the sale of power is expected to remain over Rs. 277.29 billion (lower than the Rs. 304.27 billion registered in 2001-02)[6].

The transmission and distribution losses remain abysmally high, being over 40% in some states. A significant proportion of this loss is of a non-technical nature, primarily due to theft of electricity. This is further worsened by the poor payment record of customers, a situation which keeps collection efficiency low in many states. This leads to cash flow problems for utilities resulting in delayed payments for purchased power, coal, and rail transportation. The SEB dues reached Rs. 25,727 Cr. in Feb. 2001 (GOI, 2001). The Ahluwalia committee recommendations led to a one-time settlement of SEB dues through their securitisation as state bonds in favour of the debtors. A tripartite agreement was signed to ensure that such a precarious situation would not develop in the future. In the case of the failure of a state's utilities to pay dues, the creditors can have recourse to the state's plan allocations and its share of central taxes.

A natural-monopoly-public-utility argument was used to justify government ownership of the sector, barring some exceptions. The sector retained a legal monopoly status leading to the development of vertically integrated state electricity boards (SEBs). Historically, however, there were islands of private licensees in a few urban regions. The lack of competition, accompanied by political influence and operational inefficiency, has steered the sector towards the abyss of financial distress. Persistent political interference, even in the era of 'independent' regulation, has reduced hopes for a speedy recovery. A lack of project management expertise and accountability has led to inordinate delays in planned investments and has exasperated misgivings regarding the sector. The task of bridging the capacity shortages through large-scale investments cannot be completely entrusted to public planning, which has often slipped over its targets. Policymakers recognized this in the early 1990s and opened up the sector for greater private

[6] Data on 20 major states; excluding the privatised utilities in Orissa and Delhi.

participation. Encouraged by favourable policy developments and the advent of independent regulation, greater private participation is becoming visible in the sector, though not to the extent desirable.

Table 4
Generation Capacity by Source and Ownership (in MW; on March 2006)

Ownership	Hydro	Steam	Gas	Diesel	Nuclear	Renewable	Total
State	25248	38305	3500	605	0	68	67725
Central	6172	25973	4419	0	3360	0	39924
Private	906	4241	4771	597	0	6123	16639
Total	32326	68519	12690	1202	3360	6191	124287

Note: Additional Captive Generating Capacity = 19485 MW
Source: CEA (2006a)

The existing ownership structure of the generating capacity is dominated by CPSUs and state utilities (Table 4). Only 13.4% of the generating capacity in the country is owned by the private sector. Nearly all of the inter-state transmission capacity is owned by the Central Transmission Utility (CTU), Power Grid Corporation of India Ltd. (PGCIL). All intra-state transmission capacity is owned by the respective state transmission utilities. Under a recent initiative, a joint venture between public (PGCIL) and private (a Tata group company) investor is constructing a transmission line, which is nearing completion. Other private investors such as Reliance Energy Ltd. have recently applied to the CERC for transmission licensees. Apart from the privatisation of distribution utilities in Orissa and Delhi, private distribution licensees have been operating for decades in the urban areas like Mumbai, Kolkata (Calcutta), Surat, Ahmedabad and Noida. A number of policy developments, as discussed in the next section, in the sector have emphasised the increasing role for private investors and reforms of the sector to improve its financial performance.

5

Policy Developments for Private Investment in the Indian Power Sector

The economic crisis faced by India in 1990-91 provided an opportunity for unshackling the economy by de-licensing a number of sectors. This led to the opening up of the infrastructure sectors including power and telecommunication to enhanced private participation. Sectoral policies as well as those governing foreign investment were liberalised. Sector-specific developments were aimed at improving the policy climate for private investment. The power sector has witnessed various phases of policy developments. The earliest phase, which began in the early 1990s, was aimed to improve the policy climate for private investment. Later on, the emphasis was placed on regulatory reforms leading to the establishment of independent regulatory commissions. The enactment of the Electricity Act 2003 led to a deepening up the reform process through the introduction of a competitive regime in the Indian power sector. These policy and regulatory developments are further discussed below in terms of specific policy milestones.

5.1 Private Power Policy

In 1991, the government of India amended the Electricity Supply (Act) 1948 to allow the entry of private investors in power generation and distribution. A tariff notification issued in 1992, provided for a two-part tariff structure covering fixed and variable costs. It provided for a 16% rate of return on equity at 68.5% PLF for thermal plants and (coal/lignite/gas) at 90% availability for hydro power plants. The achievement of higher efficiency levels translated into higher rate of return for investors.

5.2 Mega Power Policy

In 1995, the government strengthened its policy for private investment in generation projects over 1000 MW and which would supply electricity to more than one state, terming them as Mega power projects. The policy was intended to introduce a competitive bidding for awarding the projects. CEA, POWERGRID and NTPC were to provide catalytic support to private investors by identifying potential sites, arranging the transmission of power and for preparing feasibility report respectively. The policy did not propose any fiscal concessions. Some of these shortcomings were addressed in the revised policy of 1998 (Revised Mega Power Policy). Nineteen projects, 14 in the public sector and 5 in the private sector were declared to be mega power projects. To alleviate risks to private investors on account of payment security, the Power Trading Corporation (PTC) was setup to purchase power from the identified projects and to sell it to identified SEBs. This included the adoption of a new package of security mechanism consisting of Letter of Credit and recourse to state government's share of Central Plan Allocations. Establishment of Regulatory Commissions and privatisation of distribution in cities with a population exceeding one million were included as pre-conditions in the policy. Import of capital equipment for such projects was exempted from customs duty. The projects were also granted income tax holiday for 10 years and, which could be claimed in any block of 10 years within the first 15 years. The policy was further liberalised by according mega project status to all inter-state thermal projects of 1000 MW and above, and to all inter-state hydro projects of 1000 MW and above. These projects were now able to secure duty free import of capital goods.

Due to concerns over transparency associated with MOU-based projects, the government issued norms for tariff-based bidding for thermal power projects in 1997. Further, this role was handed over to respective regulatory commissions. These norms were to serve as guidelines, and the regulatory commissions were to issue terms and conditions for tariff and retain purview over the PPAs for sale of power to the respective state utilities.

5.3 Policy Reforms for Investment in Transmission

In addition to generation, the sector also requires substantial investment in transmission network. In order to meet the projected requirement for additional power generation capacity of 100,000 MW by 2012, the Ministry of Power estimates that the investment requirement for the inter-state transmission network will be Rs. 710 billion. A significant proportion of this (Rs. 500 billion) is expected to be undertaken by the Power Grid Corporation of India Ltd. (POWERGRID), the

Central Transmission Utility (CTU). The remainder (Rs. 210 billion) is expected to come from by private investors.

As a means to encourage private investment in transmission networks, the Electricity Laws (Amendment) Act 1998 was enacted. This facilitated the infusion of private sector investment in transmission through grant of transmission licenses. Guidelines for private sector participation in the transmission sector were introduced in January 2000. These guidelines envisage two routes for private sector participation - Joint Venture (JV) route, wherein the CTU/STU owns at least 26% equity and the balance is contributed by the Joint Venture Partner (JVP) and the Independent Private Transmission Company (IPTC) Route, wherein 100% of the equity is owned by the private entity. A joint venture for the construction of a 1200-km transmission line to transmit power from Bhutan to the Northern grid has been successfully launched by PGCIL with the Tata Group.

5.4 Regulatory Reforms

An appropriate policy framework for private participation in the power sector is a necessary but not a sufficient condition for to improve the climate for private investment in the sector. Major hurdles faced by the private investors included frustrations in receiving administrative approvals[7], payment risks with financially weak SEBs/distribution utilities, lack of sovereign guarantees,[8] political stability and the partially liberalised fuel markets, especially for the coal sector.

The government realised that in order to attract much-needed private investment into the power sector, the separation of the distribution segment of the power sector should be carried out to improve its performance. Led by similar developments in a number of countries around the world a process of reform was introduced in the state of Orissa. It became the first state to unbundle the electricity board into five corporatised entities–one each for generation and transmission, and one each for the three distribution zones in the state. An independent regulatory commission (Orissa Electricity Regulatory Commission) was also set up to oversee the functioning of the transmission and distribution companies. Orissa later privatised its power companies. Subsequently, Haryana and Andhra Pradesh also followed the twin strategy of unbundling and regulatory

[7] As discussed later, most of the license related approval requirements have been done away with. However, protracted project development process for generation projects has to undergo a number of federal, state and local level approvals that take away time and sap the enthusiasm of investors.

[8] The sovereign guarantee from the central government was last accorded to selected 'fast track' projects in 1990s. Irwin et al. (1997) has questioned the long-term presence of government guarantees.

reform. In 1998, the Central Electricity Regulatory Commission (CERC) was set up under the Electricity Regulatory Commissions Act, 1998. The main functions of the commission include regulating the tariffs of generating companies owned or controlled by the Central Government or those serving more than one state, as well as inter-state transmission and tariffs of transmission utilities.

At the state level, the State Electricity Regulatory Commissions (SERCs) introduced a transparent procedure for tariff filing, its review, and the adoption of an order under which the utilities would fix transmission and distribution tariffs for various consumer categories. The process of tariff determination has become more transparent and participatory due to public announcement of tariff filings by the utilities. This process includes organisation of public hearings and invitation for public comments thus bringing credibility to the process. In order to alleviate consumer concerns regarding quality improvement and better response by the utilities to their complaints, the SERCs have not only undertaken steps toward the formulation of complaint handling procedure by the utilities but also a system for themselves so that consumers can bring their concerns before the commission. Twenty-four states have set up regulatory commissions, and 18 of these regulatory commissions (the SERCs) have issued tariff orders. The smaller states in the North East have established a Joint Electricity Regulatory Commission. Thirteen states have unbundled and corporatised their previously integrated SEBs. Orissa and Delhi have privatised distribution. The bitter public experience and its political concerns have led other state governments to take a more cautious approach toward privatisation. The independence of regulatory institutions remains undermined by indirect control over the appointment of the members of the regulatory institutions and by delaying financial independence to such institutions. The regulatory environment has nevertheless reduced uncertainties associated with *ad hoc* behaviour by the electricity utilities under political influence. The concerns regarding regulatory uncertainty and lack of incentives in the rate of return regulation have been addressed through adoption of a multi-year tariff (MYT) framework by the CERC. The Electricity Act 2003 prescribed adoption of MYT principles by all regulatory institutions. Some of the SERCs have initiated a consultation process for introducing the same. However, its effective implementation would be influenced by availability of reliable historical data which is crucial to designing appropriate incentives.

5.5 Distribution Reforms and Privatisation

Most of the ills of the Indian power sector find its origin in the distribution segment. The distribution segment has lagged both in terms of operational efficiency as well as financial performance. The slow pace of investment generation as well as distribution segment can be attributed to the severe cash flow problem associated with the under-recovery of costs and poor collection efficiency. Poor operational efficiency further aggravates the situation. The Kohli Committee on financing of power sector emphasised the need for improving the financial viability of state utilities and for reforming the power sector in states. Without these crucial steps, it was felt that the desired investments in the power sector may not be forthcoming (GOI, 2002a).

Recognising the need to accelerate reforms in the distribution sector the central government introduced the Accelerated Power Development Programme (APDP) in 2000-01 to restore the commercial viability of the distribution segment. To encourage reforms in the distribution sector, it was rechristened the Accelerated Power Development and Reforms Programme (APDRP) during 2002-03. Additional emphasis was placed on milestones for reforming the ailing distribution segment in the states. The main objectives of the programme include - improving the financial viability of state utilities, reducing of aggregate technical and commercial (AT&C) losses, improving customer satisfaction, and increasing the reliability and quality of the power supply. The scheme also encourages the establishment of the State Electricity Regulatory Commissions (SERCs), metering of 11 kV feeders and of all consumers, and energy audits at the 11 kV level. A number of state utilities gained from the APDRP scheme by reducing cash losses and securing equivalent grants from the central government. The reform linked investment component also motivated restructuring and initiation of regulatory reforms in various states.

The privatization plan for distribution zones in Delhi specified a five-year tariff profile, agreeable to the regulator (Delhi Electricity Regulatory Commission). This helped in mitigation of regulatory risk by ensuring tariff certainty and performance milestones for a five-year window. Even so, the privatisation scheme was made possible by a substantial subsidy of USD720 million budgeted by the state government over the five year period. This would not be easy to replicate in other states. The Planning Commission estimated that if the privatisation of distribution in other states is carried out in line with the Delhi model, it would translate into a viability gap financing of Rs. 1000 billion (GOI, 2005b). In the privatized distribution zone of Orissa and Delhi, T&D losses remain above 45% and 40% respectively. Given the not-so-successful experience to date, the Planning Commission has suggested alternatives such as last mile privatisation involving metering, meter reading, billing and collection (GOI, 2005b).

5.6 The Electricity Act 2003: The Emerging Competition and Private Investment

The single buyer model, which envisages the sale of power from IPPs to financially weak state utilities/SEBs, has proven to be a hurdle to further development. After a number of drafts and amendments in the Lok Sabha and the Rajya Sabha, the Electricity Act 2003[9] came into effect from 10 June 2003. It replaces the three existing laws governing the power sector, namely, the Indian Electricity Act, 1910; the Electricity (Supply) Act, 1948; and the Electricity Regulatory Commissions Act, 1998. Apart from consolidating the laws relating to generation, transmission, distribution and use of electricity, the Act includes the following main provisions,

- De-licensing of thermal generation and removal of restrains for captive generation;
- Open access to transmission;
- Provision for license free generation and distribution in rural areas and provision for management of rural distribution by Panchayats, Cooperative Societies, non-Government organisations, franchisees etc.
- Provision for the payment of subsidies through budget;
- Setting up of an Appellate Tribunal to hear appeals against the decisions of the CERC and SERCs;
- Mandatory metering of all electricity supplies;
- Recognition of trading as a distinct activity with ceilings on trading margins to be fixed by the Regulatory Commissions;
- Phased introduction of open access in distribution and provision for surcharge until the current level of cross subsidy is gradually phased out;
- Regulatory commission to be guided by multi-year tariff principles.

The Act has enabled competition in the bulk power market through the de-licensing of thermal generation, open access to transmission and recognition of trading activity. Phased competition in the retail electricity supply will now be guided by the open access regulations for the distribution network issued by the respective SERCs. Impending competition in the distribution segment further highlights the need for improving efficiency in this segment of the power sector. This re-emphasises the acceleration of distribution reforms in the sector.

The Act also embodies policy and regulatory support for encouraging private investment in the power sector.

- Tariffs should encourage optimal investment (Sec. 61 (c))

[9] Hereinafter, it is referred to as "the Act".

- The central and the state commissions should advice the central and the state governments respectively on the promotion of investment in the electricity industry (Sec. 79 (2) (a) (iii) and Sec. 86 (2) (ii)).

An amendment[10] to the Act stipulates open access to all customers requiring maximum power above 1 MW by 27th January 2009. This opens up the market for direct sales by IPPs, bypassing the distribution licensees. As the applicable cross-subsidy surcharge is to be progressively reduced and eliminated by the SERCs, the market for electricity will open up greater avenues for prospective IPPs. New capacities to be created over the next few years would be best placed to utilise this opportunity to their advantage.

Subsequent to the enactment of the Act, the National Electricity Policy (NEP) and the National Tariff Policy (NTP) were formulated by the Ministry of Power. The National Electricity Policy (NEP) has reemphasised the role of private investment in generation, transmission and distribution. The National Tariff Policy specifies financial norms associated with the determination of reasonable tariffs to ensure financial viability and attract investment.

Increased competition and direct access[11] to consumers through open access is set to improve the investment climate. Competition is expected to bring efficiency to the market and provide incentives for cost reduction. Direct sales to customers will eliminate payment risk associated with the single-buyer model, where IPPs were only allowed to sell to the SEBs only. In order to protect the incumbent utilities from skimming of creamy layer of industrial and commercial customers by traders and IPPs, the Act provides for a cross-subsidy surcharge and an additional surcharge. The former allows for the recovery of a part of the cross-subsidy which was being provided by the customer leaving the incumbent utility. The later is to recover costs associated with stranded assets that were used to supply electricity to the consumer. Setting higher level surcharge would obviate the essence of competition. The National Tariff Policy, issued in 2006, has formalised tariffs in such a way as to restrict them to lower levels, thereby enhancing competition and facilitating direct sales to consumers.

[10] The Electricity (Amendment) Act, 2003.

[11] Investors in generation assets in Brazil face a contrasting situation. Low tariffs for large high-voltage consumers do not make it attractive for private investors even though it is theoretically feasible to do so (Rosenzweig *et al.*, 2001).

6

The Framework for Private investment in the Indian Power Sector

Policy reforms in the Indian power sector and regulatory initiatives have resulted in the emergence of a framework for private investment in generation, transmission, distribution and trading activities as outlined in the Tables 5, 6, 7, and 8 below respectively. Available information related to market entry, pricing framework and policy and regulatory framework have been synthesised from appropriate policy and regulatory documentations, and is presented in these tables.

Table 5
Framework for Private Investment in Power Generation

S. No.	Market Characteristic	Policy and Regulatory Framework
1	Customers	SEB/Distribution licensees; customers accorded open access by respective SERCs; traders
2	Entry	De-licensed thermal and captive generation; CEA's concurrence required only for hydro projects over a specified capital cost. No licensing for generation and distribution in rural areas. Built Own Operate (BOO) as well as Built Operate Transfer (BOT) framework.
3	Market (Customer) Access	Open access of inter-state and intra-state transmission; Phased open access of distribution network as specified by the respective SERCs. Access to large customers available in some states as early as April 2005; Provision for multiple distribution license (EA - Sec. 14); Distribution licensees to purchase a percentage of the total consumption of electricity in the area of a distribution licence

S. No.	Market Characteristic	Policy and Regulatory Framework
3	Market (Customer) Access	from electricity generated using renewable sources. Such percentage to be specified by the respective SERCs. (EA – Sec. 86 (1) (e)).
4	Pricing Framework for Sale to Distribution Utilities	1. New IPPs - Competitive bidding as per guidelines for competitive procurement by distribution licensees (EA – Sec. 63). 2. New IPPs – Non-competitive projects for sale to distribution licensees – To be determined by CERC / SERC as the case may be. As per terms and conditions of CERC/SERC, as the case may be. (EA – Sec. 21 (1) (a)) 3. Existing Plants owned / controlled by CPSUs and state owned generating companies (including new plants to be build up to next five years or as decided by regulatory commission as envisioned in the NTP) – As per the terms and conditions of CERC/SERC. 4. Existing IPPs and one time capacity extension up to 50% - As per existing or agreed PPA and terms and conditions of CERC/SERCs, as the case may be. 5. Distribution companies to buy a certain percentage of their power purchase from renewable sources – Price determined by the SERCs. 6. Transactions due to real time imbalances as per the frequency-linked charge for unscheduled interchange (UI) under the ABT framework.
5	Pricing Framework for Sale to Open Access Customers	For direct sale by any generating company / trader to customers granted open access – as per mutual agreement. (EA – Sec. 49) Subject to cross-subsidy surcharge and additional surcharge to be determined by the respective SERC.
6	Financial conditions for tariff determination for generating companies	Rate of Return on Equity -14% (post tax) D/E Ratio – 70:30 Target availability for recovery of full capacity (fixed) charges - 80% Incentive –25 paise/kWh for ex-bus scheduled energy corresponding to scheduled generation in excess of ex-bus energy corresponding to target Plant Load Factor of 80%. Operational and financial norms notified by CERC.
7	Subsidy	No direct subsidy burden – To be provided directly to the distribution licensee by the respective state government, if it desires to subsidise a consumer or class of consumer.
8	Cross-subsidy	Only in case of sale to open access customers – Cross-subsidy surcharge and additional surcharge. Cross-subsidy surcharge to be eliminated by SERCs in phases. Cross-subsidy surcharge not applicable in case of consumer switching to another distribution

S. No.	Market Characteristic	Policy and Regulatory Framework
8	Cross-subsidy	licensee. i.e. If generator also secures distribution license of the area, it avoids payment of cross subsidy or additional surcharge.
9	FDI	100% foreign equity permitted[12]; through automatic route[13]
10	Policy Framework	Private Power Policy 1991 Mega Power Policy 1995 (Revised in 1998 and 2003) Electricity Act 2003 National Electricity Policy National Tariff Policy National Electricity Plan Ministry of Power guidelines
11	Regulatory Framework	Relevant regulations issued by the Central Electricity Regulatory Commission and the respective State Electricity Regulatory Commissions as per applicable jurisdiction.
12	Other Related Agencies	Appellate Tribunal for Electricity Central Electricity Authority (CEA) Inter Institutional Group to facilitate financial closure of projects Central Transmission Utility (CTU) - Power Grid Corporation of India Ltd. State Transmission Utilities (STUs) Regional Load Despatch Centers (RLDCs) State Load Despatch Centers (SLDCs) Regional Power Committees
13	Future Developments	Power market development and emergence of Merchant Power Plants. Initiative for Five Ultra Mega Projects for 20,000 MW capacity. Scope for Regional Power Projects for import of electricity in the country

[12] Government of India Gazette Notification No. 237 dated 22 October 1991. It has been further clarified by the Ministry of Finance that the condition of dividend balancing by export earnings which is normally being applied to cases of foreign investment up to 51% equity will not be applicable in this case.

[13] Projects for electricity generation, transmission and distribution with foreign equity up to 100% had been made eligible for automatic approval (other than atomic reactor power plants) (Press Note No. 7/2000 dated 14 July 2000, Ministry of Commerce & Industry, Department of Industrial Policy & Promotion).

Table 6

Framework for Private Investment in Inter-state and Intra-state Transmission

S. No.	Market Characteristics	Policy and Regulatory Framework
1	Customers	SEB/Distribution utilities and open access customers – for short-term and long-term transmission/wheeling of electricity;
2	Entry	Licensed by CERC (inter-state transmission)/SERCs (intra-state transmission) Two routes for private sector participation - (i) the Joint Venture (JV) route, wherein the CTU/STU owns at least 26% equity and (ii) the Independent Private Transmission Company (IPTC) Route, wherein 100% equity is owned by the private entity.
3	Market Access	In concurrence with Central Transmission Utility (CTU) (inter state)/State Transmission Utility (STU) (intra-state)/RLDC/ SLDCs
4	Pricing	CERCs Terms and Conditions for Tariff – current conditions applicable till March 2009. Regional postage stamp basis with normative D/E ration of 70:30 Guided by National Tariff Policy
5	Framework for Return	Rate of Return on Equity - 14% (post tax) Target Availability for recovery of full transmission charges (AC system - 98%; HVDC – 95%). Incentives – on prorate basis for availability above the target availability for the transmission system. Return on Foreign Equity - Equity invested in foreign currency is allowed a return in the same currency and payment is made in Indian Rupees on the exchange rate prevailing on the due date of billing. Operational and financial norms notified by CERC.
6	Subsidy	No direct subsidy burden.
7	Cross-subsidy	No direct cross-subsidy burden - (indirect influence through revenue stream of the distribution licensee)
8	FDI	100% foreign equity permitted through Independent Power Transmission Corporation (IPTC) route. As JV with local CTU/STU holding up to 26% stake in the transmission company
9	Policy Framework	Guidelines for Private Investment in Transmission, 2000 Tariff based Competitive-bidding Guidelines for Transmission Service, 2006

S. No.	Market Characteristics	Policy and Regulatory Framework
9	Policy Framework	Guidelines for Encouraging Competition in Development of Transmission Projects, 2006 Electricity Act 2003 National Electricity Policy National Tariff Policy Ministry of Power guidelines National Electricity Plan
10	Regulatory Framework	Relevant Regulations issued by the Central Electricity Regulatory Commission and the respective State Electricity Regulatory Commissions as per applicable jurisdiction
11	Other Agencies	Appellate Tribunal for Electricity Central Electricity Authority (CEA) Empowered Committee constituted by Min. of Power Central Transmission Utility (CTU) - Power Grid Corporation of India Ltd. State Transmission Utilities (STUs) Regional Load Despatch Centers (RLDCs) State Load Despatch Centers (SLDCs) Regional Power Committees
12	Future Developments	A transmission pricing that takes into account distance and direction in addition to the quantum of power flow (National Electricity Policy).

Table 7
Existing Framework for Private Investment in Distribution

S. No.	Market Characteristics	Policy and Regulatory Framework
1	Customers	End consumers; other state utilities
2	Entry	Distribution License for Urban areas issued by SERCs. Provision for Multiple Distribution License. Distribution (including generation) in rural areas is de-licensed. Distribution Licensees can appoint franchisees for operations within their license area.
3	Market Access	Third party access through phased open access by SERCs. Provision of multiple distribution licensees by the SERCs.

S. No.	Market Characteristics	Policy and Regulatory Framework
4	Pricing Framework	Rate of Return on Equity - 14% (post tax) Retail tariff determined by SERC under Rate of Return Regulation. Multi-year tariffs (MYT) framework to be introduced by SERCs[14]. Access to distribution network priced by the SERCs. Third party access attracts a cross-subsidy surcharge and additional surcharge to be determined by the respective SERC. Cross-subsidy surcharge to be eliminated by the SERCs in a phased manner. In case of multiple distribution licensees, SERCs may fix only a maximum limit on tariffs (EA – Sec. 62(1)(d)).
5	Financial conditions for tariff determination	Rate of Return - NTP specifies a rate of return on equity of 14%. SERCs can consider higher return for the distribution business due to increased risk to investors. Operational and financial norms notified by respective SERC.
6	Subsidy	To be provided in advance by the state government to subsidise any consumer or class of consumer. (EA – Sec. 65)
7	Cross-subsidy	Industrial and commercial consumers cross subsidise domestic and agricultural consumers. SERCs to reduce and eliminate cross subsidy in a phased manner. (EA – Sec. 39)
8	FDI	100% foreign equity permitted; through automatic route.
9	Policy Framework	Private Power Policy Electricity Act 2003 National Electricity Policy National Tariff Policy Ministry of Power guidelines (for competitive procurement and bidding)
10	Regulatory Framework	State Electricity Regulatory Commissions
11	Future Developments	Multi-year Tariff Privatisation of distribution utilities formed after restructuring of erstwhile SEBs. Performance based regulation.
12	Other Agencies, Programs	Appellate Tribunal for Electricity Grievances Redressal Forum and Ombudsman Accelerated Power Development and Reforms Programme (APDRP) – targeted at efficiency improvement and reduction of losses of distribution utilities. Rajiv Gandhi Grameen Vidyutikaran Yojana (for Rural Electrification)

[14] Introduced by the Andhra Pradesh Electricity Regulatory Commission (APERC) from 2006-07 for a three year control period.

Table 8
Framework for Private Investment in Inter-state and Intra-state Trading

S. No.	Market Characteristics	Policy and Regulatory Framework
1	Entry	License by CERC (for inter-state trading) / SERCs (for intra-state trading)
2	Market Access	License for annual trading volume linked to net worth of the licensee in accordance with trading regulations issued by CERC/SERCs.
3	Pricing	For trading under competitive bidding, there is no regulation of price. For negotiated trading transactions, the maximum trading margin on inter-state trading has been fixed by CERC at 4 paise per kWh. Margin for intra-state trading.
4	Rate of Return	No rate of return assured for trading activity. Cap on maximum margin for negotiated trades.
5	Subsidy	No direct subsidy burden.
6	Cross-subsidy	For sale to distribution licensees - No direct cross-subsidy burden - (indirect influence through revenue stream of the distribution licensee due to cross-subsidisation of the tariff for certain category of consumers) For sale to open access customers – Cross-subsidy surcharge and additional surcharge determined by the SERCs.
7	Policy Framework	Electricity Act 2003 National Electricity Policy National Tariff Policy Guidelines for competitive procurement by distribution licensees
8	Regulatory Framework	Relevant regulations issued by CERC / SERCs, especially those related to trading and open access.
9	Future Developments	Market Development initiatives such as Power Exchange that would allow futures and spot trading. Regional Electricity Market encompassing electricity trade with neighbouring countries.

As per the National Tariff Policy, new projects to be undertaken by the CPSUs/state generating companies during the next five years need not undergo the process of competitive bidding. Tariffs for such projects would be determined by the CERC/SERCs under the prevailing rate of return framework (GOI, 2006). This offers a window of opportunity for foreign investors as minority stakeholder in such projects.

A number of crucial policy initiatives have been put in place to create an enabling environment for private participation. The immediate concern for the Indian power sector is to improve the performance of distribution utilities as this influences payment security for private investors in generation and transmission projects. The development of a power market would also help improve investment climate. If designed properly, power markets provide efficient signals for investment and offer an alternative market in case of payment problem with the state utilities. Investors also face tough challenge in negotiating through the bureaucracy (Table 9). Power projects require ten statutory and four non-statutory clearances (GOI, 2005c).

Table 9
Bureaucratic Hurdles to Doing Business

	Enforcing a Contract		Starting a Business	
	Days	Procedures	Days	Procedures
India	425	40	89	11
PRC	241	25	41	12
Argentina	520	33	32	15
Brazil	566	25	152	17
Thailand	390	26	33	8
Mexico	421	37	58	8
Best Practice	48 (Netherlands)	14 (Norway/UK)	5 (USA)	2 (Australia/ New Zealand)

Source: World Bank (2005c)

Although policy reforms and growth prospects were able to generate interest from private investors in the power sector in the 1990s, bureaucratic delays often frustrated investors' efforts and many project proposals fell through. In spite of such hiccups, private investors have acquired a stake in the growth of the Indian power sector. The following section reviews the state of private and foreign investment in the sector.

7

Status of Private and Foreign Investment in the Indian Power Sector

7.1 Private Investment in the Indian Power Sector

The economic crisis facing the country in the early 1990s opened up opportunities for private, including foreign investment, in the Indian power sector. The Private Power Policy 1991 opened up the path to private and foreign investment in the generation and distribution of electricity. Private investors were offered a 16% return on equity,[15] which was further incentivised in the case of higher efficiency levels in terms of plant load factor (PLF). The policy framework for private investment was further strengthened through the introduction of the Mega Power Policy in 1995 for thermal projects over 1000 MW and hydro projects over 500 MW. This was revised in 1998 and a number of fiscal incentives were added for large power projects. Initially, these initiatives generated overwhelming initial interest from local as well as international private investors. However, the insolvency of the sole buyer, the SEBs, and delay in project development frustrated the efforts of private investors. Clearly the investors were not finding the assured 16% return on equity[16] to be commensurate with the risk of investing in the sector at that time. They sought the comfort of sovereign guarantees, which were limited to eight fast track projects, a misnomer. Enron's Dhabol power plant, which was one amongst them, has been riddled with controversies since it was first agreed upon. The controversial PPA, which was lopsided in the favour of project developers, was renegotiated amidst a political drama[17]. It later fell into

[15] In line with the market scenario, CERC has reduced the allowable return on equity to 14 % (CERC, 2004).

[16] Due to PLF-linked incentives, the effective rate of return on equity may be higher than this.

[17] Following the global collapse of the parent company, Enron Inc., and contractual disputes, the project has recently been rescued and restarted by a consortium of Indian public sector companies.

serious trouble when the parent company Enron faced trouble back home. The controversy has recently been settled after the foreign investors' stake was purchased by a SPV created by state-owned companies.

Growth in the power sector since independence has been primarily accompanied by public investment through economic planning. As a result of this, most of assets in the electricity sectors are owned by government-owned companies or the SEBs. The erstwhile SEBs own about 55% of the generating capacity followed by the central sector generating companies, which are owned by the central government. Since the policy liberalisation in 1991, 39 private projects[18] totalling 7417 MW capacity have been commissioned by December 2005. This includes 1495 MW capacity installed by the existing private distribution licensees. Most of the distribution network is owned by the state utilities. A few urban areas, some of which have been licensed to private companies for nearly a century, and the distribution companies in Orissa and Delhi, are under majority private ownership. The transmission segment is dominated by public ownership with the exception of the upcoming public-private joint venture for importing electricity from the Tala hydroelectric project in Bhutan. Given the limited fiscal space[19] for increasing investment by the central as well as state governments, and requirements for future investment, there is a greater scope for private participation in the sector.

Table 10
Privately Owned Generation Capacity and its Share (As on 31st Dec. 2005)

Regions	Total Capacity (MW)	Private Capacity (MW)	Percentage Share
Northern	33782	571	1.69
Western	34868	5793	16.61
Southern	35819	5212	14.55
Eastern	16681	1565	9.38
North-eastern	2443	26	1.07
All India	123668	13187	10.66

Source: CEA (2005b)

The geographical distribution of private power projects in the country reveals a preference for the southern and western regions of the country (Table

[18] A list of private projects commissioned since the policy liberalisation in 1991 is given in Appendix A.

[19] The desire for prudential fiscal and debt management led to enactment of the Fiscal Responsibility and Budget Management Act 2003. The act sets time-bound target for reduction in fiscal deficit of the government.

10). Investors' choice[20] of a particular state is influenced, among others, by the relative investment climate in the state, the growth potential, the financial status of the buyer utility and the available risk mitigation options. The investment climate is influenced by the policy and regulatory framework, including various incentives offered by the state government. Given the federal and state structure of the Indian political system, the states often compete amongst themselves to offer better investment climate for investors. VENKETESAN & VARMA (1998) observe that following central government's liberalization of investment in the power sector, there is evidence of competition among states to provide better incentives for attracting private investment. Some states have managed to maintain a sustainable investment environment for the investors. This has kept the investors' interest alive in the power sector in more hospitable states (Lamb, 2005).

The relative dominance of states in the southern and western regions could be explained as follows. In terms of financial and operational performance, and reform parameters, power sector in the states of Andhra Pradesh Gujarat and Karnataka have been rated amongst the best in recent years (Table 11). In terms of overall investment attractiveness, the states of Maharashtra, Andhra Pradesh, Karnataka, Tamil Nadu and Gujarat have been rated top five destinations by foreign investors (FICCI, 2002; 2003).

A number of private projects have been commissioned since the process of liberalisation began in the early 1990s. However, this is insufficient to address the burgeoning capacity shortage in the country. The risks associated with poor financial state of state utilities has kept private investors at bay. The Electricity Act 2003 and a number of recent policy initiatives have re-established some faith in the Indian power sector. To facilitate faster project development, a proposal has been made for setting up five ultra mega power projects of 2000 MW each. So far, requests for qualification (RFQ) have been invited for two such projects. The Power Finance Corporation, a domestic financial institution catering to the power sector, is entrusted with the responsibility of initial project development. These projects are to be offered to investors on an internationally competitive basis.

The investors perceive relatively higher risk for investment in the distribution segment, which is characterised by inefficiency and are exposed to regulatory risk. The limited experience of distribution privatisation in Orissa and then in Delhi also fails to present encouraging results. Distribution, being a state issue, is highly influenced by local political dynamics. Since privatisation would suggest an increase in tariffs and less space for inefficiency, there is resistance from

[20] Ideally, one needs to analyse the factors influencing the location of private investment in greenfield power projects across various Indian states. This is outside the scope of the present study.

within and without these organisations. Due to the poor financial status of most of the state utilities, the privatisation of distribution requires support by the respective state government. In the case of privatisation of distribution companies

Table 11
Top Five Rated State Utilities (2003 to 2006)

Rank	2003	2004	2005	2006
1	Andhra Pradesh	Delhi	Andhra Pradesh	Andhra Pradesh
2	Karnataka	Andhra Pradesh	Gujarat	Gujarat
3	Haryana	Goa	Delhi	Delhi
4	Rajasthan	Karnataka	Karnataka	Karnataka
5	Maharashtra	Gujarat	Tamil Nadu	West Bengal
6	Delhi	Haryana	Goa	Goa
7	Gujarat	Punjab	Himachal Pradesh	Himachal Pradesh
8	Himachal Pradesh	Himachal Pradesh	West Bengal	Pradesh
9	Tamil Nadu	Uttar Pradesh	Uttar Pradesh	Maharashtra
10	Punjab	Rajasthan	Chattisgarh	Kerala

Source: CRISIL/ICRA (2006, 2005, 2004, 2003)

(Discoms) in Delhi, the state government committed a support of about Rs. 35000 million to the private investors over a period of five years against benchmarks for efficiency improvement, in terms of the reduction of Aggregate Technical and Commercial (AT&C) losses. The Planning Commission has noted that similar financial package for the privatisation of Discoms in other states would require support of Rs. 1 trillion (GOI, 2005b). Improving the financial and technical performance of the state utilities would be an effective alternative to this financial dole. More recently, a number of state distribution companies have shown signs of turnaround, as seen through improvements in various financial and technical benchmarks. This is a positive sign for prospective investors in greenfield generation assets and for future privatization of these Discoms in future.

7.2 Foreign Investment in the Indian Power Sector

Globalisation of the economy has led to increase in cross border trade as well as investment in developing countries. FDI inflows to developing countries have increased in line with the improved investment climate, higher corporate earning and liberalised rules for foreign ownership (World Bank, 2005b). However, significant regional disparities are evident. South Asia recorded much lower inward FDI as compared to East Asia, Latin America and East Europe. In 2004,

Table 12
Country Wise Foreign Direct Investment (FDI)
and Foreign Technology Cases (FTCs) Approved (from Aug. 1991 to Mar. 2005)

		No. of Approvals			FDI Approved (millions)		Percent-age
S. No.	**Name of Country**	**Total**	**Tech-nical**	**Finan-cial**	**(In Rs)**	**(In USD)**	
1	Australia	3	0	3	17.65	0.38	0
2	Austria	5	3	2	146.13	4.25	0.03
3	Belgium	6	2	4	2861.48	85.36	0.65
4	Canada	2	0	2	651.05	15.19	0.15
5	Cayman Island	7	0	7	37889.8	1044.26	8.63
6	PRC	3	2	1	5	0.12	0
7	Denmark	4	1	3	358.6	7.82	0.08
8	Finland	6	0	6	1621.02	43.31	0.37
9	France	10	3	7	450.66	11.41	0.1
10	Germany	25	2	23	8794.39	245.96	2
11	Hong Kong	3	0	3	4196.4	101.08	0.96
12	Ireland	1	0	1	55	1.31	0.01
13	Isle of Man	4	0	4	1200.88	30.41	0.27
14	Japan	11	4	7	3614.3	84.12	0.82
15	Korea (South)	9	2	7	32364	832.27	7.37
16	Malaysia	14	0	14	35842.4	949.15	8.16
17	Mauritius	84	3	81	94468.1	2426.54	21.5
18	NRI	24	1	23	7668.05	212	1.75
19	Netherlands	4	0	4	108.6	3.03	0.02
20	Norway	1	1	0	0	0	0
21	Oman	1	0	1	5	0.14	0
22	Panama	1	0	1	6142.5	171.24	1.4
23	Poland	1	1	0	0	0	0
24	Russia	1	0	1	0.51	0.01	0
25	Singapore	9	0	9	4829.88	131.9	1.1
26	Spain	4	0	4	1095.42	26.08	0.25
27	Sweden	3	1	2	84.63	1.88	0.02
28	Switzerland	4	1	3	6.69	0.15	0
29	U.A.E.	1	0	1	1.61	0.03	0
30	U.K.	38	2	36	52258.2	1490.07	11.9
31	U.S.A.	120	7	113	137140	3873.48	31.22
32	Ukraine	1	1	0	0	0	0
33	Unindicated Country	5	0	5	5407.2	149.94	1.23
	Grand Total	**415**	**37**	**378**	**439285**	**11942.9**	**100**

Source: Personal communication with Department of Industrial Policy & Promotion, Government of India (June 2005) these regions recorded FDI inflows of USD63.6 billion, 42.4 billion and 37.6 billion, respectively, as compared to just USD6.5 billion in the South Asian region (World Bank, 2005b).

Liberalisation of the Indian economy in the early 1990s was aimed at attracting both private domestic as well as foreign investment. The policy framework for FDI in the power sector is designed to offer unhindered flow of capital from outside the country. It provides for 100% FDI in the power sector through an automatic route. The total number of approvals for foreign investment and the investment by source country[21] are given in Table 12.

From the data presented in the table above, it is not possible to ascertain the actual foreign investment flow[22] in the sector, which might differ from the investment approved. Table 13 below provides information on actual FDI inflows in the sector during the period 2000 to 2005.

Table 13
Actual FDI Inflows in Power Sector (2000-05) (Rs. million)

	2000	2001	2002	2003	2004	2005	Total	Total (USD billion) #
FDI in Power Sector	4760.2	8225.1	30494.6	1907.4	2510.6	1518.5	49416.2	1.1
Total FDI Inflow	100923.1	158418.9	161233.5	95640	147813.7	192707.2	8567365	19.04
Share of Power Sector (in %)	4.72	5.19	18.91	1.99	1.7	0.79	5.77	5.77

Source: Department of Industrial Policy and Promotion, Government of India
Note: # - At exchange rate of @ Rs. 45 / USD approx.

It should be noted that the actual FDI amount to approx. USD1.1 billion whereas approvals since 1991 were a staggering USD12.9 billion. Though the data is not

[21] Due to the favourable taxation treaty with Mauritius, significant investment is routed through that country. The data does not show the original country of origination of the investment.

[22] To the dismay of the research community as well as other interested parties, statistics on actual FDI inflow in the power sector was not compiled separately until 2000. Prior to this, the available statistics relates to 'approvals' and to a wider definition of the 'energy sector'. The other statistical challenge is on due to the absence of segregated data in terms of green field investments, purchase of government assets, investment in listed shares, investment in equipment manufacturing etc.

directly comparable due to difference in the time period, it does provide some insight into the agony of the investors', whose efforts were probably frustrated during the process of project development.

The recorded FDI inflows to the Indian economy are much lower than those recorded by some of the fast growing economies like PRC. This is partly attributed to the adoption of different definitions of FDI across nations (HENLEY, 2003). In the Indian context, the definition of FDI includes investment only through - (i) Financial collaborations, (ii) Joint ventures and technical collaborations, (iii) Capital markets via euro issues and (iv) Private placements or preferential allotments. The investments by the Foreign Institutional Investors (FIIs) in the capital market are excluded. The emerging growth theory has led to significant investment in the Indian stock markets. Some of the listed power sector companies have witnessed significant interest from the FIIs (Table 14). This speaks only about the private and the professionally managed companies owned by the central government. The NTPC earns returns in a regulated environment and is exposed to a very limited payment risk since the tri-partite agreement on SEB dues was concluded. The BHEL's attractiveness is attributed to the fact it has easy access to a relatively protected and growing market. It continues to enjoy a preference in the equipment procurement by the CPSUs.

Table 14
Holding of Foreign Institutional Investors in Listed Power Sector Companies (in %)

	Sector	Majority Ownership	30th June 2004	31st Dec. 2004	31st Dec. 2005	31st March 2006
NTPC	Generation	Public	–	4.84	6.86	7.07
BHEL	Equipment Manufacturer	Public	23.04	20.56	22.07	22.42
Reliance Energy	Generation & Distribution	Private	14.20	17.73	18.22	16.16
Jai Prakash Hydro	Generation	Private	–	–	3.59	3.79
CESC	Generation & Distribution	Private	13.71	15.08	17.20	19.19

Note: # - 30th June 2005
Source: Online data from the National Stock Exchange, Mumbai; accessed in April 2006. http://www.nseindia.com

Portfolio investments of the kind reflected in the above table reflect positive sentiments toward the sector but these are not a sustainable means for attracting financing to the sector. Such investments are also subject to volatility and do not significantly assist in sustainable asset addition in the sector.

While the sustainability of large public investment in the sector is desirable, there is growing need for investment in other social sectors like health, primary education etc. Apart from this, the concerns for management of government finances leave much to be desired from the private sector. In order to meet the long-term growth requirements of the sector, the sustainability of private and foreign investment is also desirable. This, however, is influenced by a number of factors - policy and regulatory environment, legal framework, and financial attractiveness. This is further discussed in the following section.

8

Factors influencing Private Investment in the Power Sector in Developing Countries: The Role of the Policy Environment and Regulatory Reforms

The natural-monopoly/public-good argument has long provided a pretext for governments to maintain public ownership of the power sector, especially in developing countries. The lack of investment and poor efficiency of the sector, along with changes in the lending policy of the multilateral development institutions, led to reforms in the sector. The reforms programs are undertaken to develop a conducive environment for private investment in the sector. An improvement in the technical and financial performance of electric utilities is also an intended outcome of the reform program even while the utilities remain under public ownership. In some cases, divestiture of public assets is aimed at achieving this objective.

The flow of private capital from developed to developing economies is influenced by higher expected returns and the growth potential of developing markets. The investors can choose from a basket of opportunities in various countries and across a number of sectors. The factors influencing this decision are classified as follows,

(i) Country Specific Factors - These include macroeconomic fundamentals, growth potential and political stability. These influence a country's risk premium and, hence, the foreign investment. Apart from this, foreign investment is often restrained by policies that regulate the flow of capital, repatriation of capital and dividends earned thereof. The political risk continues to remain a major hurdle for investment in infrastructure sectors in developing countries. Macroeconomic crises leading to significant currency depreciation in the East Asian and the Latin American countries have raised concerns for macroeconomic stability in developing countries.

(ii) Sector Specific Factors – These include policies that influence industry structure, entry, competition and pricing behaviour in the sector under consideration. These factors along with policy and regulatory environment influence the financial viability of projects. The independence, scope and jurisdiction of regulatory institutions also influence the returns that the investors can make and risks thereof. The design of regulatory framework and market institutions, especially for the power sector, influence competition and adequacy of investment in the sector. The cross-sectoral issues like liberalisation of fuel markets (i.e. coal, natural gas etc.) also effect investment in power generation projects. In the existing Indian context, fuel allocation to power projects and its pricing has a great bearing on financial viability and financial closure of greenfield investment in generation assets.

(iii) Project Specific Factors – These include a number of contractual issues (such as Power Purchase Agreement, Fuel Supply Agreement, land acquisition, environmental issues etc.). These are linked to the legal framework of the country. The bureaucratic delays stretch the project development process and often frustrate investors' sentiments. The maturity of domestic capital market influences the ability of developers to raise long-term debt at a reasonable cost. Payment risk remains a major hurdle to private investment in the Indian power sector.

The country specific factors determine the overall attractiveness of a country for foreign investment and also influence the international lenders' willingness to participate in a project. The policy interventions, with adequate commitment from the government, generally yield results over a period of time. Infrastructure projects with long-term exposure to investors are particularly vulnerable to country specific factors, which influence global investment trends. The sector specific interventions like liberalisation of investment and sectoral reform are initial signals for private investors. The continuity and consistency of this process, which may include tariff reforms and privatisation, are often influenced by political factors. This takes toll of sustainability of investment in the sector. The project specific factors, which are part of project development process, consume a significant effort of investors. The ability of project developer to hedge risk rests on the policy and regulatory framework. These are often addressed through legal contracts among various stakeholders: investors, lenders, utilities, government and consumers. These issues are often ironed out through a negotiation process, especially in the early phase of private investment in the sector. However, it is not a substitute for a transparent framework for private investment.

The investors' concerns related to sector as well as project specific factors have been addressed through establishment of an independent regulatory institution. The role of independent regulation is to provide a justifiable rate of return to investors while protecting consumers' interest. The creation of such regulatory institutions along with legislated private sector participation in the sector is aimed at mitigating risks associated with long-term investment in the sector. The policy and regulatory environment play a crucial role in promotion of private and foreign investment in the sector (STERN & CUBBIN, 2005; SIRTAINE *et al.*, 2005; KIRKPATRICK *et al.*, 2004; ESTACHE, 2004; PARGAL 2003).

WOODHOUSE (2005a), from a study of nine countries, identifies five key factors that constitute the investment climate for private investment in the power sector: (i) strong public finances, (ii) viability of the sector, (iii) efficiency of fuel markets, (iv) political climate including the role of civil society and (v) the legal framework. A survey of international investors in the power sectors of developing countries reveals that while assessing country conditions, investors give priority to (LAMECH & SAEED, 2003) (i) Legal framework that defines investors' rights and obligations; (ii) Payment discipline and enforcement and (iii) availability of a guarantee from the government or a multilateral agency. The following four factors seem to represent the mindset of Japanese investors in making decision for investment in the power sector of developing countries[23] - sovereign guarantees, a strong local partner, demand growth and the rate of return.

Foreign investment in the infrastructure sector in developing countries responds positively to the presence of an effective regulatory framework that provides regulatory creditability to the private investors (KIRKPATRICK *et al.*, 2004). While examining the relationship between the quality of regulatory framework and foreign investment, KIRKPATRICK *et al.* (2004) find that weak regulatory institutions and those vulnerable to "capture" by the host governments dilute the commitment of investors to large projects.

In another study using data on 155 developed and developing countries during the period 1995 to 1997, GLOBERMAN and SHAPIRO (2002) conclude that governance infrastructure is an important determinant of both inward as well as outward FDI. An able governance infrastructure not only attracts capital, but also enables an environment under which domestic multinational corporations emerge and invest abroad. Further, the authors find that investments in governance infrastructure are subject to diminishing returns. Hence, its benefits for FDI inflows are more evident for smaller and developing economies.

[23] Personal interview with TEPCO officials in November 2005.

In a study conducted for ADB, NERA (1998) follows trends in regulatory governance across six developing countries over a period of 10-15 years. The study finds an improvement in regulatory effectiveness across various infrastructure sectors including electricity[24], natural gas, telecom, transport and the water sector. However, there was neither a similar speed of regulatory reforms nor there was a convergence towards a common solution or towards best regulatory practices. STERN & CUBBIN (2005) review a number of studies evaluating the effectiveness of regulatory institutions and governance arrangements for the electricity industry, more particularly in the context of developing countries. The authors conclude that there is evidence for the literature suggesting effectiveness of regulatory agencies in promoting investment in the electricity sector. The authors also highlight the role of well-designed industry structure, transparent and reliable legal system, and commercialization, especially in pricing as key issues in the success of regulatory reform and independent regulation.

The economic literature related to emerging infrastructure policy issues in developing countries highlights the importance of governance and corruption in the sector (ESTACHE, 2004). Transparent policies and independent regulatory agencies bring in a semblance of governance to the sector. A transparent policy framework and effective legal system help to protect property rights of investors. Corruption remains a key concern in improving the technical and financial performance of the sector. Property rights and bureaucratic quality also influence private investment in infrastructure sector (BANERJEE *et al.*, 2005). Countries that have succeeded in attracting financing for infrastructure projects have taken care of following legal aspects (KUMAR *et al.*, 1997) – (i) establish a system for protecting private investment, (ii) create mechanisms for parties to bind themselves through contracts and (iii) provide for enforcement of agreements reached.

An empirical analysis of a panel data spanning two centuries for over 100 countries leads HENISZ (2002) to conclude that policy environments that limit the feasibility of policy change are a key determinant of infrastructure investment. The author also suggests that policymakers should pay heed to the structure of political institutions and that any shortcoming should be compensated, if necessary. Such gaps are often addressed through incentives for investment and sovereign guarantees. From an empirical study, PARGAL (2003) finds that a legislation for liberalizing private investment, regulatory certainty and independent regulatory bodies are critical determinants of private investment flow to the infrastructure sector in Latin American countries.

[24] The electricity sector was studied in the case of Bangladesh, India, Pakistan and the Philippines.

In the absence of a favourable policy environment that permits cost recovery, government guarantees or other forms of financial support, privatization of public assets is possible. The investors adequately discount the value of the assets they are purchasing and hence achieve an acceptable level of returns. This is, however, not feasible in the case of greenfield investments in new projects, and failure on the part of the governments to provide a conducive policy and regulatory environment leads to a demand for government guarantees and other financial support (DAILAMI and KLEIN, 1997).

Many developing countries with weak investment climate continue to provide government guarantees, which typically include payment and/or revenue guarantees. Other kind of support from government as well as multilateral institutions comes in the form of credit enhancement mechanisms like maturity extension, performance based grants etc. (KUMAR *et al.*, 1997). The sovereign guarantees[25] are not a substitute for an effective policy and regulatory environment. This has often been used as an instrument of comfort in the early phase of opening up of the power sector for private investors. Business risks, including those associated with variations in exchange rate and interest rate, should best be covered by the private investors rather than government providing a guarantee[26] cover for the same (KLEIN, 1997). Transparent and predictable government policies obviate the need for sovereign guarantees (IRWIN *et al.*, 1997; KLEIN, 1997).

Effective regulation - supported by law; financial autonomy and decision autonomy - should be a key priority to protect both the interests of consumers and investors (SIRTAINE *et al.*, 2005). The failure of early IPPs in Mexico is attributed to a lack of a regulatory environment (PROTEGO, 2000). An independent regulatory institution strengthens an effective policy implementation. This may not completely eliminate government guarantees, but could help reduce its scope and scale. Government support may still be required for viability support for many infrastructure projects including power supply schemes for poor and rural consumers.

An investor survey finds that 48% of the foreign investors felt that the prevailing regulatory system across various economic sectors in India was average

[25] USAID (1995) explores seven alternatives to the sovereign counter-guarantees in the Indian case. These include a World Bank guarantee facility, export credit agency guarantees, Indian bank financing/guarantees, state government guarantees, escrow accounts with receivables from creditworthy industrials, power wheeling, and traditional corporate balance sheet financing.

[26] Klein (1997) suggests the establishment of a centralised agency for managing the government guarantee programs. This would help institutionalise cost-benefit analysis of guarantee programs and these can be limited to a monetary limit on government's exposure. Like multilateral development agencies, governments' guarantee program should include a policy for appropriate guarantee fees and coinsurance requirements. This would provide appropriate incentives for risk reduction by investors.

with 52% rating it as below average (FICCI, 2002). The survey identifies the following factors, which are critical to the growth of FDI inflows in India. These include: (i) Political stability; (ii) Reduction in ground level obstacles; (iii) Market growth; and (iv) Manpower. In a subsequent survey by FICCI (2003), the investors rated the following four factors to be the critical in determining future FDI growth in the Indian economy: (i) Stability in policy guidelines; (ii) Reduction in ground level obstacles; (iii) Political stability and (iv) Rate of return. These two surveys emphasise that policy certainty and political stability are major factors influencing future FDI growth in the Indian economy. This is a fitting explanation for the infrastructure sectors as well. The desire of investors for higher rate of return also stems from risk associated with uncertainties related to political instability and policy uncertainty. The ground level administrative hurdles extend the project development phase and take a toll on investor sentiments.

8.1 Independent Regulation and Private Investment in Power Sector

Using data from a study by Estache and Goicoechea (2005), we find a positive correlation between independent regulation and private investment in the generation and distribution segment (Figs. 5 and 6). The influence seems to be more pronounced in the case of investment destined for the distribution segment. While 73% of the Latin American countries have independent regulatory institu-

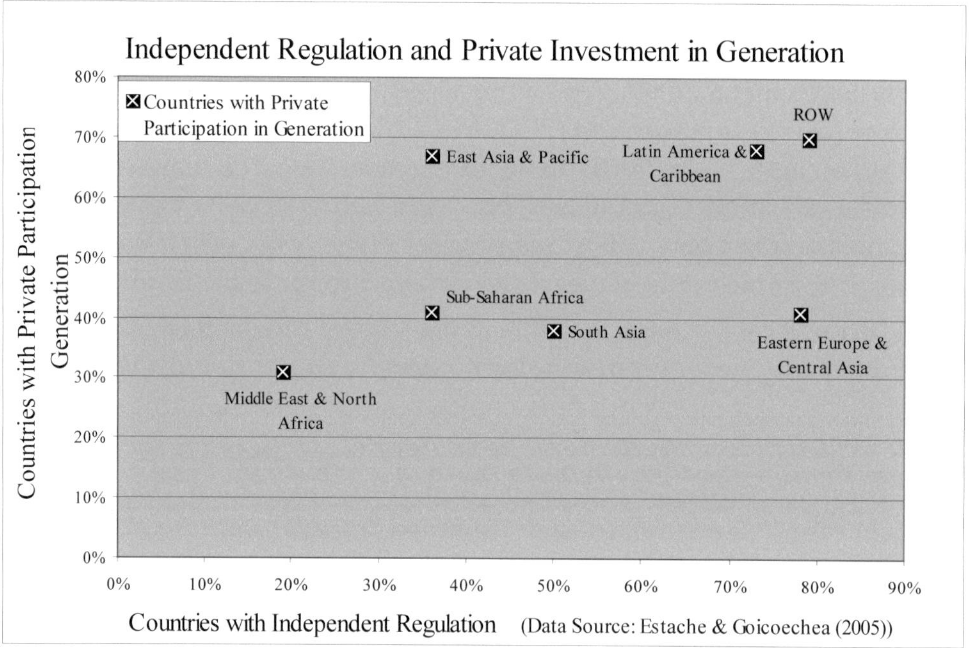

Fig. 5 Independent Regulation and Private Investment in Power Generation

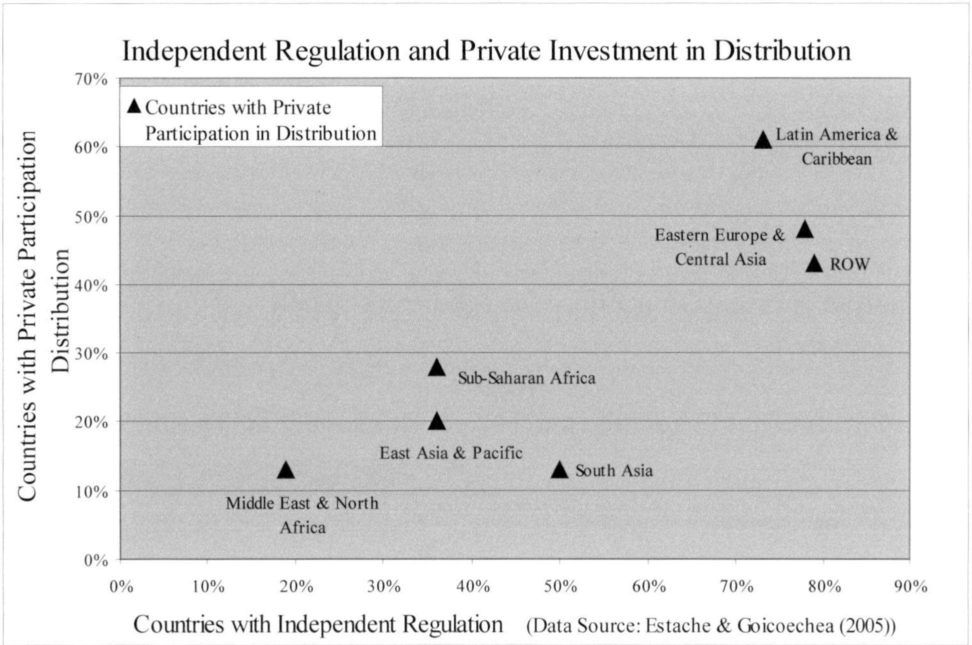

Fig. 6 Independent Regulation and Private Investment in Power Distribution

tions, only half of the South Asian countries would qualify under this criterion. In this background, the percentage of countries with private participation in generation was 68% and 38% respectively in the Latin American and South Asian region. Private participation in the distribution segment was recorded lower at 61% and 13% in the two regions respectively.

The figures present a proxy representation. It would be more appropriate to ascertain if countries with independent regulation are able to attract private investment in generation and distribution than those without it. This analysis is discussed as follows.[27] The private investment in generation and distribution is more likely to coexist with an independent regulatory institution in the power sector. In the absence of independent regulation, private participation in distribution (Table 16) is not as encouraging as in the case of generation (Table 15). This, however, does not conclusively demonstrate whether independent regulation leads private investment or otherwise.

The experience with private investment in various countries also suggests a greater role of an independent regulatory regime. While Argentina and Brazil

[27] It is not possible to ascertain if independent regulation was an outcome of a "design" (i.e. before inviting private participation) or a "necessity" (i.e. after private participation took place). This could be a potential area for further research.

Table 15
Independent Regulation and Private Investment in Generation

	Independent Regulatory Agency		
Private Investment in Generation	Yes	No	NA
Yes	**59**	18	7
No	27	**49**	4
NA	9	3	31

Note: Analysis of the data from Estache and Goicoechea (2005)

Table 16
Independent Regulation and Private Investment in Distribution

	Independent Regulatory Agency		
Private Investment in Distribution	Yes	No	NA
Yes	**51**	5	3
No	36	**60**	4
NA	8	5	38

Note: Analysis of the data from Estache and Goicoechea (2005)

witnessed an increase in private investment in the presence of a regulator, PRC witnessed gradual investor pullout due to its absence. Private investment in the PRC was welcomed as early as in the late 80s. The uncertainty associated with the FDI approval process, electricity sector regulation, and the risk of default on power purchase contracts continue to be the most significant institutional barrier for FDI investment in the PRC's power sector (Blackman & Wu, 1999). The absence of an independent regulatory institution and frequent tariff revisions made investors wary of prospects in the 1990s. This later also led to exit of investors from the country (Woo, 2005b).

The literature reviewed in the previous section and the above analysis point out the importance of a transparent policy environment and independent regulatory framework in attracting private investment in the power sector in developing countries. Although a number of developing countries, including India, have undertaken regulatory reforms, the outcome in terms of attracting private investors varies. This seems to be a necessary rather than sufficient condition. The transition path and sustainability of reforms provide long-term policy stability, thereby reducing investors' risk perception. There is a clear trend towards more effective regulatory governance in the electricity sector in India. However, it is difficult to ascertain a convergence of regulatory regime to the best practice, which itself is difficult to define (NERA, 1998). The timing and sequencing of the reform program seem to have cast a large influence on the investors' interest. The following section investigates some of these aspects through a comparative policy analysis between India and five selected countries.

9

Policy and Regulatory Environment in India: A Comparative Analysis with Argentina, Brazil, PRC, Mexico and Thailand

The liberalisation of the power sector in India began with the opening the sector to private investment in 1991. Argentina and Brazil opened up their markets in 1992 and 1995 respectively. However, in spite of being an early bird, the Indian power sector was not successful in attracting private investment as compared to these two countries. Apart from commercial attractiveness, a different approach to reforms and the evolving policy framework and regulatory structure seem to have influenced the outcome. A comparative analysis is required to further analyse these aspects. In order to understand the relative strengths and weaknesses of the power sector reform and investment climate for private investors in India, it would be useful to compare it to a peer of countries that have "successfully" attracted substantial private investment in the power sector. We have selected Argentina, Brazil, PRC, Thailand and Mexico for such an exercise[28]. As discussed later, the countries selected represent a wide spectrum of model for private participation and reform in the power sector. The first two have a significant share of private investment in the power sector. The PRC is included on account of its overall FDI attractiveness. The last two, namely, Thailand and Mexico have been considered "best practices" for the IPP model (Woodhouse, 2005a).

Tables 17 and 18 provide comparative information on key attributes of the power sector and policy environment across six countries. These tables are partly

[28] Some of the other countries to have attracted substantial private investment include the Philippines, Indonesia, Malaysia, Morocco, Turkey, Columbia, Chile and Pakistan. We, however, limit the scope of our analysis to the selected countries only.

Table 17 Key Attributes of the Power Sector in

	Argentina			Brazil			PRC		
	1993	1998	2003	1993	1998	2003	1993	1998	2003
Size of the System (MW)	NA	23470	25000	NA	65135	92179	NA	277000	353000
Households with an Electricity Connection (%)	NA	95	NA	87 (1991)	92	95	NA	97	99
Hours of Power Outages from Public Grid @	22 (1992)	6 (1995)	NA	NA	NA	NA	NA	NA	NA
Av. Residential Elec. Tariff $	41 #	NA	33 #	NA	0 .099	0.22	NA	0.05 -0.07	0.05-0.08
Av. Industrial Elec. Tariff $	2430.7 #	NA	2124.9 #	NA	16.82	0.099	NA	0.05-0.09	0.05-0.09
Trans. and Distr. Losses (in %)	18 (1993)	8 (1998)	NA	15.24	15.2	16.28	NA	8.1	7.7
Subsidies	Y			Y (for large consumers)			NA		
Cross-subsidies	Y			Y (-tve)			Y (for large state-owned enterprises)		
Competitive Bidding Since	NA			Y (1995)			Proposed		
Wholesale Market	1992			1998			---		
Access to Eligible Consumers	2000			1995			---		

Source: Compiled by the Author from various sources
Notes:
- in Local Currency Units (LCUs); $ - Nominal USD/kWh;
* - Energy and Peak shortages (in percentage) assessed for connected load.

Selected Countries: A Comparative Analysis

	India			Mexico			Thailand		
	1993	1998	2003	1993	1998	2003	1993	1998	2003
	69065 (1992)	85795 (1997)	107877	32010	34978	40520	NA	17261	25945
	42.17 (1991)	NA	55.8 (2001)	NA	95	NA	NA	82	84
	7.8/18.8 (1991-92) *	8.1/11.3 (1997-98) *	7.5/12.6 (2001-02) *	7.45	2.53	NA	NA	27	21
	77.27	136.18	244.55	0.2009	0.4367	0.8459	0.07	0.06	0.06
	171.5	312.73	420.19	0.1815	0.3965	0.7508	0.064	0.05	0.06
	19.8	24.79	31.53	18.43 (1992)	20.89 (1999)	16.71	NA	8.7	7.3
	Y			Y - Govt. Budget			NA		
	Y (phased reduction stipulated in Electricity Act 2003)			Y			Y		
	Limited (1995)			Y			Y		
	Enabled in 2003			N			N		
	2005			N			N		

Table 18 Policy Environment for Private Investment

	Argentina			Brazil		
	1993	1998	2003	1993	1998	2003
Reform Philosophy	Unbundling → Privatisation of Discoms → Wholesale Market – retail access			Unbundling → Privatisation of Discoms → Wholesale Market – retail access		
Commercialisation and corporatisation of the state owned utility.	N?	Y	Y	N	Y	Y
Enactment of an energy/electricity law permitting unbundling and privatisation.	Y	Y	Y	N	Y	Y
A regulatory body separate from the utility and ministry	Y	Y	Y	N	Y	N
Private sector investment on greenfield sites.	Y	Y	Y	N	Y	Y
Restructuring/separation of the core state owned utility.	Y	Y	Y	N?	Y	Y
Privatisation of an existing state owned enterprise.	Y	Y	Y	N	Y	Y
Private investment in the sector permitted since		1992			1995	
Sectors open for private investment	G, T, D	G, T, D	G, T, D	–	G, T, D	G, T, D
Model for private participation		Divestiture Concessions			Divestiture Concessions	
Electricity market context for IPPs		privatized electricity market, selling in competitive contract & spot markets.			partially private electricity market, selling to distribution companies and large users.	

Source: Compiled by the Author from various sources
Notes: G - Generation, T - Transmission, D - Distribution; Tr - Trading;

in Selected Countries: A Comparative Analysis

PRC			India			Mexico			Thailand		
1993	1998	2003	1993	1998	2003	1993	1998	2003	1993	1998	2003
Private Participation → Unbundling → Regulatory Reforms			Unbundling → Regulator → Part Divestiture of Discoms → Competitive Bulk and Retail Supply			Unbundling → Wholesale Market → Privatisation			Unbundled Sector; No Regulator; A proposal for competitive power pool was dropped in 2003		
NA	Y	Y	N	Y	Y	N	N	N	N	N	N
NA	N	N	N	N	Y	Y	Y	Y	N	N	N
N	N	Y	N	Y	Y	N	Y*	Y*	N	N	N
NA	Y	Y	N	Y	Y	Y	Y	Y	N	Y	Y
NA	N	Y	N	Y	Y	N	N	N	y	y	y
NA	Y	Y	N	Y	Y	N	N	N	N	Y	Y
1985			1991			1992			1994		
G	G	G	G, D	G, T, D	G, T, D, Tr	G	G	G	G	G	G
BOT			Divestiture BOO			BOO			BOT		
reforming electricity market, selling to provincial power authorities.			reforming electricity market, could sell only to SEBs until 2003.			unreformed electricity market, selling to vertically integrated national utility.			unreformed electricity market, selling to national generation and transmission utility.		

* - Regulatory authority does not approve retail tariffs, which are approved by the Ministry of Treasury.

adopted from ADB *et al.* (2005)[29] and are expanded to include additional parameters from a variety of sources and updated with information for 1993. The evaluation of policy and regulatory developments in the Indian power sector and the comparative policy analysis with five selected countries (presented in Table 17), enable us to derive following inferences about factors influencing private investment in the Indian power sector.

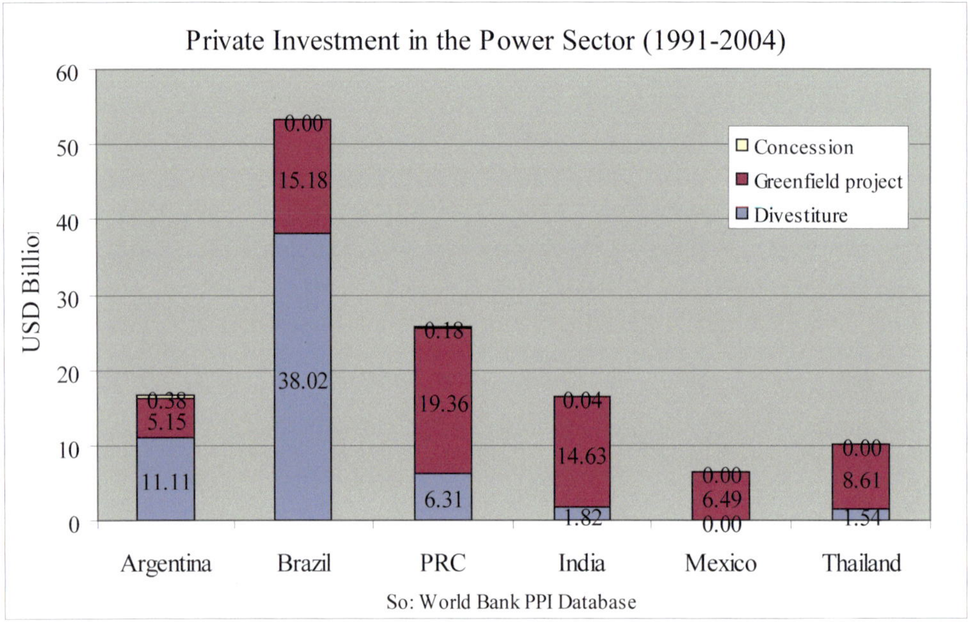

Fig. 7 Private Investment in the Power Sector: A Cross-country Comparison

9.1 Pace and Sequencing of Reforms

The process of liberalisation of private investment and power sector reform varies across the countries in terms of pace as well as sequencing. The transition from the initiation of sectoral reforms to the point, when the rules of the game for private investors are clear, is identified as a fundamental constraint to private investment in the power sector (ROSENZWEIG *et al.*, 2001). ZHANG *et al.* (2004) found that setting up an independent regulatory authority before privatisation is expected to boost generation capacity while introducing competition before privatisation, improves capital utilisation in the sector.

The initial phase of private investment in Argentina was dominated by privatisation of distribution utilities. Argentina also adopted across the board re-

[29] This information was available for 1998 and 2003 only.

form by setting up an independent regulator and introduction of a wholesale electricity market in 1992. This seems to have significantly boosted the privatisation program. It also provided a commercial environment for purchase of electricity on competitive basis. Later on, this also paved way for emergence of merchant power plants in Argentina.

The privatisation program in Brazil was dominated by partial divestment of distribution utilities through competitive bidding in 1995. This was aimed at attracting new investment at competitive costs. By 1998, Privatization of 19 distribution and 4 generation companies netted USD 22.18 billion. Receipts from privatisation of distribution utilities netted USD 19.43 billion (OLIVEIRA, 2003). In order to provide incentive to domestic distribution companies, access to consumers was also permitted. This provided the much needed incentive to distribution utilities for improving their performance. An independent regulatory body was setup in 1996. Beginning with the privatisation and regulatory reforms, the wholesale power market took shape only by 2003. This delay, together with other uncertainties, limited the appetite for greenfield investment in power generation (MILLAN *et al.*, 2001).

The Mexico adopted a cautious approach to private participation in the power sector. From the historical experience with banking transportation and telecommunication sector, privatisation was considered a taboo. Significant level of subsidies and low tariffs for electricity also made it politically difficult to make attempts in this direction (NÚÑEZ-LUNA, 2005). The IPP investors in Mexico and Thailand had relatively more secure power purchase contracts with largely government owned electric utilities. In both the case, the IPPs were also provided certain fuel supply risk cover through state owned gas companies (NÚÑEZ-LUNA, 2005; WOO, 2005a). Public electric utility, the *Comisión Federal de Electricidad*, in Mexico undertook exchange risk upon itself by promising payment in foreign currency and bearing risk arising out of fuel supply (NÚÑEZ-LUNA, 2005).

The Mexico and India share quite a few similarities in terms of private sector experience and challenges to reform in the power sector. The power sector in both the countries is dominated by public utilities and faces significant political resistance to privatisation. Consumer tariffs in both the countries are subsidised and are supported through government budget. Mexico opened up the power sector for private investment in 1992, a year after India did so. However, the first financial closure for a power project in Mexico materialised only in 1998. Private investment in Mexico is solicited through competitive bidding to sell electricity to the incumbent utilities. In contrast to this, most of the private projects in India have been negotiated. The competitive bidding evolved slowly in India and witnessed low enthusiasm in the case of distribution privatisation in Orissa and

Delhi. A regulatory institution for the sector was setup in 1995 in Mexico. The regulatory reforms picked up gradually in the Indian context beginning with the setting up of the first state level regulatory institution in Orissa in 1995. The federal regulator, the CERC, was established in 1998. Investment in the Mexican power sector materialised in a competitive manner and after a regulatory institution for the sector was in place. This highlights the importance of regulatory reforms in attracting private investment. The slow investor response in the Indian power sector could be attributed to higher risks on account of lack of transparency and absence of an independent regulatory institution.

The experience with the selected countries suggests that regulatory reforms should precede or immediately follow the policy for liberalising private investment. Delays in keeping up with policy and regulatory reforms after the opening of the sector to private investors, along with administrative hiccups, seem to have sapped investors' enthusiasm in the Indian context. In spite of the early opening of the market, subsequent policy and regulatory reforms were slow to evolve. Limited experience in dealing with the private sector in a number of states and bureaucratic hurdles delayed project development. After the sector was opened for private investment in India in 1991, the first experience with independent regulation came about four years later in 1995. It took 12 years for enacting a legislation (the Electricity Act 2003) to usher in an era of competition in the sector. The lack of a roadmap in the initial phase keeps uncertainties alive for investors. The process of reforms in the power sector needs to follow a logical conclusion by creating a sustainable climate for investment. Before embarking on privatization and encouraging a private investment, the following order of reforms is suggested (IIE, 2002) - establish a sound regulatory framework, restructure government assets, and organize market rules. Further the distribution reforms should precede liberalisation in the generation segment. We have been holding the stick from a wrong end. The urgency is to address the ills of the distribution segment through a strong political will by state governments and a commitment to perform by the distribution utilities.

9.2 Financial Viability of Distribution Utilities

Distribution companies with poor operational efficiency, especially high T&D losses, create an imbalance in the financial sustainability of the sector. Unless there is rapid improvement in operational efficiency, significant tariff hikes are required for meeting the revenue requirements of distribution companies. This makes the process of reforms and privatisation politically unpopular, and puts it at the vagary of the prevalent socio-political situation. A combination of three strategies is often used to postpone tariff hikes. First, the state owned distribution companies do not seek significant tariff revision and borrow funds to bridge the financial gap. Second, state governments provide additional subsidy support to avoid tariff hike for politically sensitive class of consumers. This translates into additional borrowing for the state governments or diversion of funds from other socially desirable sectors. In some cases, regulators have resorted to creation of a 'regulatory asset', which postpones tariff hike for future tariff reviews.

In the case of Argentina, where T&D losses were initially high, the improvement came about relatively quickly. It declined from 26% in 1991 to 7% by 1999 (CEE, 2006). In the early phase of reforms, Brazil emphasised improvement of the financial situation of the utilities and prepare them for privatization. This was accomplished through enactment of Law 8631 and by allowing utilities to raise prices and eliminating policy of cross subsidisation from low cost utilities to high cost utilities. Apart from this, an incentive based 'price-cap' tariff scheme replaced the 'cost-of-service' regime for all concessions in the sector, thus allowing utilities to profit from efficiency gains.

An improvement in efficiency of distribution companies also addresses payment security concern of the IPPs thereby improving investment climate in the sector. In the Indian context, incumbent utilities are to face competitive pressure to retain large industrial and commercial customers in the next few years due to phased open access to customers as permitted by the respective SERCs. Due to limited fiscal space for subsidies, improvement in the financial performance of the incumbent state utilities through reduction in AT&C losses and rationalisation of tariffs becomes more desirable.

9.3 Addressing Political Risk

Political risk overshadows private investment in power generation as well as privatisation of distribution utilities. In the Indian context, most of the political risk would usually arise on account of influence of state-level politics on the contracts signed by the distribution companies as experienced in the case of Dhabol project. Given the ongoing economic reform process in the Indian economy, political risk at the federal level remains limited to political instability that may influence the direction of reforms itself. For projects involving foreign investment, political risk could be addressed through political risk insurance coverage provided by MIGA. Opportunities for credit enhancement mechanism for the domestic investors are usually limited to the payment security and guarantees provided by the state governments. Given its influence on the availability of plan funds to state government, the federal government may also institutionalise national level political risk insurance scheme.

From the experience in Argentina and Brazil, it is evident that performance improvement of the privatised distribution companies plays a critical role in attracting greenfield private investment in power generation. Private investors in greenfield generation assets seem to derive better comfort in dealing with the private buyer entities, which can be expected to adhere faithfully to contracts and are not prone to political changes[30]. Private entities are expected to be more reasonable than their public counterparts in negotiating power purchase deals. Divestiture of the electric utilities in Argentina and Brazil not only signalled less political intervention but also provided a reasonable counterparty for the IPP investors. Transparent rules for providing subsidies and defining cross-subsidies also limits political role in the reform in the power sector[31].

In Mexico, political resistance to reform and privatisation was compensated though additional risk undertaken by public utilities for e.g. foreign currency and fuel supply risk. The commercialisation of distribution companies can be the next alternative to divestiture. However, continued political interest in the sector inhibits ability of distribution companies to function in a commercial manner. Governments should help create commercial conditions for distribution companies by distancing themselves from commercial decision making and limiting their role to desired interventions for the identified consumer classes through subsidy support. However, this is difficult to do, given the governments are prone to changes in political regimes. Arguments in favour of the divestiture of public utilities emerge when government ownership continues to hamper the ability of the distribution companies to work on commercial principles.

9.4 Policy Stability and Independent Regulatory Institutions

Transparent and stable policies and, independent regulatory environment are effective substitutes for guarantees, which are on the vane in the sector. The guarantees are often required to safeguard against unpredictable risks. The credible policies and predictable regulation that provide a clear medium-term roadmap of reforms for the sector help in mitigating risk for investors. The IPPs in Argentina flourished in a strong market under a stable regulatory regime (Núñez-Luna and Woodhouse, 2005). The absence of an independent regulator, administrative hurdles and the risk of default on power purchase contracts especially with respect to tariffs are identified as the most significant institutional barrier to FDI

[30] Woodhouse (2005) identifies Andhra Pradesh as a positive outcome for the investor as well as for the country. A skewed PPA, which was renegotiated in the case of an IPP in Tamil Nadu makes it worse outcome for both the investor as well as the country

[31] It may, however, itself be difficult to arrive at a reasonable level of subsidy or a rationalisation of cross-subsidies.

in the power sector in the PRC. (Woo, 2005b; Blackman & Wu, 1999). Greater private participation requires an adequate regulatory framework, including a competent regulatory authority. Even where such institutions are in existence, they often lack adequate capacity (Briceno *et al.*, 2004).

The advent of independent regulation in the power sector is aimed at reducing risks for private investors in a sector that has long been dominated by the government as policy maker, regulator as well as the investor. However, 'independence' of such institutions has been questioned especially in the early phase of power sector reforms in developing countries. GOI (2005b) raises reservations about efficacy of independent regulation in the Indian power sector. It notes that lack of transparency in selection procedure, delayed, inconsistent and deficient orders and lack of accountability on the part of regulators is hampering its ability to meet the intended objectives of regulatory reforms. Most of the countries continue to exercise influence on selection of the regulators, a few requiring the presidential consent. A limited regulatory experience in developing countries often makes it desirable to appoint regulators, who have prior experience with the regulated entities. The political appointees often compromise independence of regulatory institutions. This makes it difficult to implement relatively unpopular but desirable steps such as raising tariffs for sensitive class of consumers and taking measures to improve efficiency. This dampens the pace of distribution reforms and harms the long-term interest of the sector.

With the onset of regulatory institutions, utilities are exposed to what is termed as regulatory risk. This arises due to investors' exposure to changes in the policy environment and regulatory principles, which remain unpredictable. The rate of return regulation exposes an investor to the change in regulatory approach between tariff reviews. The CERC has put in place a multi-year tariff regime for inter-state generators and transmission service providers under its purview[32]. This addresses some of the investors' concerns for stability of the tariffs and the performance standards. The concerns about regulatory risk are more pronounced in the case of SERCs. This influences investment in generation, transmission and distribution segment within the state. The uncertainty in setting performance standards, especially the T&D losses, and the specifying consumer tariffs significantly influence the risk exposure for the investors in the power sector. This was a critical concern in the case of the privatised distribution companies in Orissa. Some of these concerns have been addressed in the case of privatisation of the distribution companies in Delhi through adoption of a multi-

[32] Prior to Electricity Act 2003, the CERC introduced a multi-year tariff regime that specifies performance standards and a tariff framework for a four-year tariff review period for the licensees under its purview.

year profile for AT&C loss reduction. The multi-year tariff regime, as suggested by the Electricity Act 2003 and under consideration by some of the State Electricity Regulatory Commissions, is expected to address such concerns related to regulatory risk.

9.5 Macroeconomic Stability

Investment in the power sector involves a long-term commitment from investors, who expect to repay debt and earn return over the life of the project. The stable macroeconomic policies support foreign investment inflow in developing countries. Foreign investors are exposed to additional risk arising out of foreign exchange variation. Unless such risks are pass-through under a power purchase agreement, lenders and investors expose themselves to macroeconomic instability. A severe economic crisis, leading to significant depreciation of the currency or spiralling inflation, makes it politically difficult to absorb the associated risk through an increase in tariffs. The economic crisis in East Asia and Latin America adversely affected investors' interest not only in the afflicted countries but across developing countries, in general. The concerns about macroeconomic instability expose foreign investors to risk in developing countries, and make it difficult to bring lenders on the table. This highlights the role of fiscal prudence and financial reforms in developing countries.

10

Framework for Return and Private Investment in Developing Countries

Investors respond to the trade-off between risk and return. They seek returns commensurate with the risk of doing business in the power sector in developing countries. The flow of domestic capital to the power sector is influenced by the perceived returns and the project horizon, which tends to be relatively longer for power projects. In addition to this, foreign investors also need to cover risks associated with foreign exchange fluctuations and its repatriation. In order to attract private investment, the power sector has to compete with other economic sectors, which may offer attractive returns with shorter project horizons and

Table 19

Cost of Capital and Return on Investment in Energy Sector Projects (in %)

	Cost of Capital (WACC)	Cost of Equity	Shareholder IRR	Project IRR	Return on Capital Employed (RoCE)
Estache and Pinglo (2004) (Dev. Countries)	10.7 - 15.6	14	---	---	---
Sirtaine *et al.* (2005) (Latin America)	15	19	- 45 - 25 @	-20 +20 (@)	7.2
Sirtaine *et al.* (2005) (Argentina)	14 - Dist. 13 - Gen.	19 - Dist. 17 - Gen.	---	---	---
Sirtaine *et al.* (2005) (Brazil)	19 - Dist. 14 - Gen.	19 - Dist. 17 - Gen.	---	---	---

Note: @ - with terminal value

have relatively acceptable risk profiles. In this context, we review some of the literature related to the cost of capital and rate of returns framework for infrastructure sector especially the power sector in developing countries.

Based on a survey of investors in the power sector in developing countries, LAMECH and SAEED (2003) find that nearly 44% respondents are looking for over 16% return on their investment in the power sector in developing countries. The studies discussed below help to explain this response from investors. Investors' experience in markets liberalised for private investment reveals that the return to investors is lower than the cost of investment in the energy sector, including the power sector (Table 19). In a study using data of 120 corporations in 31 developing countries from 1998 to 2002, ESTACHE and PINGLO (2004) find that the average cost of capital varies from about 8.5% to over 14% across regions and across infrastructure sectors. East Asian countries exhibit the lowest cost of capital (about 8.5%), while it is estimated to be 14% for the South Asian region. The cost of capital for energy projects varies between 10.7% in upper-income countries to 15.6% in low-income countries. The cost of equity for the energy sector is estimated to range from over 13% for upper middle-income countries to about 19.5% for low-income countries. Against this, the return on equity[33] for energy sector in low income, low middle income and upper middle income countries were estimated to be 5.1%, 7.6% and 1.1% respectively. The study finds that the rate of return on equity, for infrastructure projects in general, falls short of the cost of equity in most regions. The East Asian region fared the best and has recovered significantly since the East Asian crisis, giving a boost to infrastructure investment in the region. After the East Asian economic crisis, only 32 out of 120 infrastructure companies in the sample were able to earn a return of equity larger than their cost of equity. The return on equity, an accounting measure of return, is influenced by accounting practices and can be significantly influenced by the sample of years under study. Not being an IRR analysis, the period of analysis may in fact include a few bad years.

ESTACHE and PINGLO (2004) also acknowledge that knowledge gaps, especially those related to accounting practices, need to be addressed through further research. These limitations are addressed to some extent by SIRTAINE *et al.* (2005) in a study of infrastructure concession projects in the Latin American countries. Return on equity as well as shareholder IRR are found to be lower than the cost of equity for energy concessions in the region. A few energy concession projects are able to generate returns (IRR) above their cost of equity even if future eco-

[33] A more-relevant comparison would be in terms of the IRR of the project. Sirtaine *et al.* (2005) analyse the IRR of infrastructure projects in Latin America. This is discussed later in the section.

nomic growth is maintained and if they are able to generate a terminal value at the end of the concession contract. The authors find that 75% of energy concession projects remain unattractive in terms of shareholder's IRR even after considering a terminal value. The study estimates the project IRR to be around -20% without considering any terminal value. However, after considering a terminal value, the project IRR exceeds the weighted average cost of capital (WACC). The authors conclude that infrastructure investments remain a risky proposal and hence require high rate of return. Regulation is an important issue in aligning[34] the cost of capital and the rate of return, and hence influences the profitability of investment (SIRTAINE *et al.*, 2005).

The low return to investors in Latin American concession projects (Sirtaine *et al.*, 2005) further highlights the importance of reducing sectoral risks through policy clarity and a more enabled regulatory structure. Investors identify the following as the most important factors for the success or failure of investment in the power sector in developing countries (Lamech and Saeed, 2003),

(i) The retail tariff level and collection discipline.
(ii) Fair adjudication of tariff adjustments and disputes.
(iii) Operational control and management freedom.
(iv) Regulatory commitment sustained through a long-term contract.

Investors' poor experiences, either on account of macroeconomic crisis or on account of unenforceable/renegotiated contracts, has reduced the appetite for investors towards the power sector in developing countries. In spite of the high risk and low tariff margins, higher growth prospects have attracted private investors to the Chinese power sector. This has been attributed to 'Can't afford not to be there' syndrome (CROW, 2001). In PRC, the IPPs were offered a guaranteed return on equity of about 15 % for 1994-97 and 10-15% for 1998-2001 (WOO, 2005b). For a number of upcoming power generation projects in PRC, return on equity is estimated to be 15-17% (WORLD BANK, 2000). The newly established State Electricity Regulatory Commission in PRC has introduced annually renewable Power Purchase Agreements (PPAs) for IPPs. Such unfavourable policy measures and the uncertainty of future developments have led to the exit of foreign IPPs from the power sector there. The fate of earlier negotiated PPAs remains doubtful in the emerging scenario (WOO, 2005b).

Prior to 2004, the rate of return on equity[35] for projects approved by the CERC in the India was fixed at 16% (CERC, 2000). This has been lowered to 14% for

[34] It was also found that regulation favours consumers more by keeping tariffs lower and avoid excess IRR over WACC.

[35] Post tax, at 80 % PLF for thermal and 90 % availability for hydro power plants.

the current tariff review period (2004-09) in accordance with market conditions (CERC, 2004). The incentives for higher plant load factor (PLF) translate to additional return for investors. Given the higher risk premium attached to sovereign rating for the Indian economy and the international experience discussed above, the returns in the Indian context may not be sufficient to attract foreign investors. Further, the distribution sector exhibits higher risk to investors than that in the generation and transmission sector. This has not been duly acknowledged by the most of the SERCs, which continue to offer this lower rate of return for equity to distribution licensees.

The poor financial strength of the distribution utilities and the politicisation of the sector continue to pose a high risk to private investors in the Indian power sector. It is believed that the politicisation of the sector, especially in terms of tariffs has not provided adequate returns to investors and this has resulted in a decline in investment in private infrastructure projects in developing countries (World Bank, 2005a). From a survey of investors in the power sector in developing countries, it is found that 60% of foreign investors were dissatisfied with their investment in India and 80 % respondents do not rate India as an investment prospect (Lamech and Saeed, 2003). The only solace is to be found in the fact that the study was probably conducted before the enactment of the Electricity Act 2003, which further deepens the reform process and addresses some of the investor concerns. A number of SERCs have permitted phased direct access to large customers[36]. Such initiatives hold greater promise to investors and will help catalyse greater investment in the sector.

The discussion presented so far in this section points to the inadequacy of returns in the Indian power sector compared to the risks present in the sector. National Electricity Policy (NEP), issued by the Ministry of Power, also notes

> "Return on investment will, therefore, need to be provided in a manner that the sector is able to attract adequate investments at par with, if not in preference to, investment opportunities in other sectors. This would obviously be based on a clear understanding and evaluation of opportunities and risks. An appropriate balance will have to be maintained between the interests of consumers and the need for investments." (GOI, 2005a)

The business of electricity distribution in India is characterised by higher risk on account of high T and D losses, poor operational efficiency and low revenue collection. The NEP observes that distribution licensees, due to high commercial

[36] USAID (1995) suggested this as one of the alternatives for the provision of sovereign guarantees.

risk in this segment of the power sector, could be provided higher returns than the prescribed 14 % for the generating plants. The SERCs need to ponder on this issue and build an incentive compatible framework to offer higher returns to the distribution licensees. This can be linked to a reduction in technical and commercial losses, and an improvement inn productivity and quality of service. The APDRP scheme[37], which provides incentives for loss reduction to the state utilities, excludes private licensees from its ambit. Until the implementation of a multi-year tariff regime, such incentives are rather limited in the existing regulatory framework in most of the states. Unless adequate returns are provided to investors in the sector, the interest of consumers will be defeated as they will continue to experience unreliable and inadequate electricity supply over the long-run due.

[37] This is discussed in section 5.5.

11

Mode of Private Participation in the Power Sector

Power sector offers a wide scope for private investment through change of ownership of existing assets or greenfield investment in generation, transmission or distribution assets. Some of the major avenues for private participation in the sector are

- Partial or full divestiture of generation and distribution assets,
- Greenfield generation or transmission assets on merchant, built own operate (BOO), built operate transfer (BOT) or, built lease transfer (BLT) basis,
- Rehabilitation of existing generation assets on build, rehabilitate, operate, and transfer.

Divestiture of generation and distribution assets is expected to bring efficiency improvement and superior management skills in the sector. However, this does not translate to capacity expansion or increased access to electricity in the immediate future. The government gains in terms of divestment funds, which can be utilised for temporarily bridging the fiscal gap. These funds can also be ploughed back to the sector or utilised for budgetary support to other social sectors.

The basket of choice available to private investors depends on the privatisation/investment liberalisation process adopted by the respective governments. There is wide variation in the mode of private privatisation among the six countries (Fig. 8). Argentina and Brazil offered a number of generation assets and distribution utilities on outright sale or partial divestment in the beginning of the reforms process (Fig. 9). The former adopted full divestiture route in most cases, whereas the later adopted more cautious approach by partially divesting government owned utilities. In contrast to this, greenfield investment through BOO route dominated private investment in India, Mexico and Thailand. Private investment in the PRC materialised through BOT that would require transfer of assets to the government agency after an agreed period. The merchant power plants differ from BOO/BOT projects in terms of absence of any power purchase agreement. Mature markets provide enough confidence to investors in merchant power plants. Argentina witnessed emergence of merchant power plants.

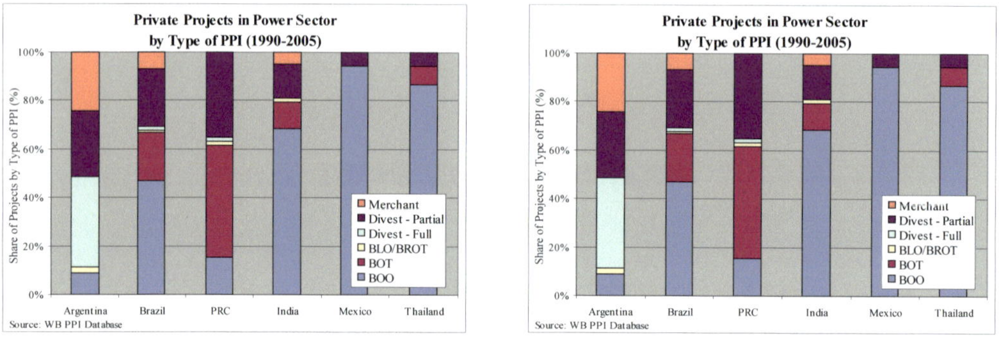

(i) (ii)

Fig. 8 Mode of Private Participation in the Power Sector

The sequencing of reforms and liberalisation program influences the mode of private participation. The risks associated with various modes of private participation and the associated expected returns also influence the level of participation. Establishment of a wholesale power market in Argentina, in 1992, was accompanied with the divestiture of the generation assets, thereby providing a number of potential players for the wholesale power market. As the wholesale power market matures,

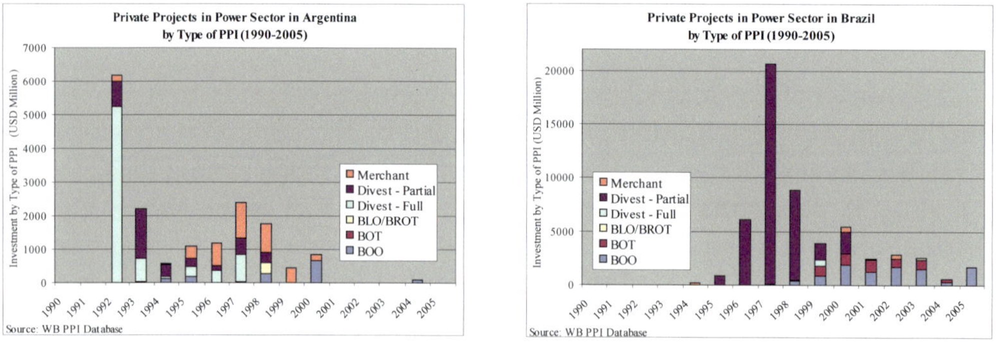

(a) (b)

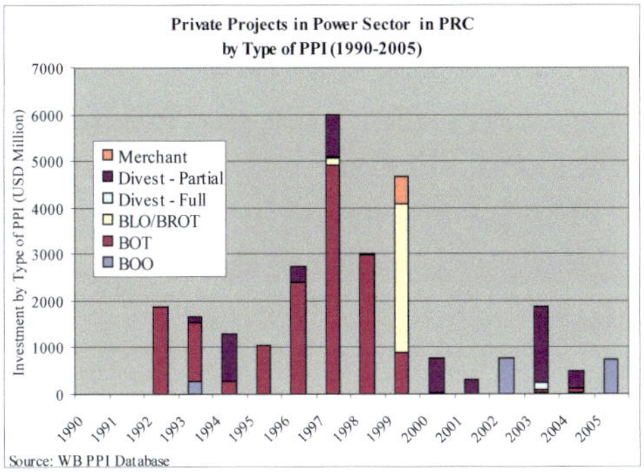

(c)

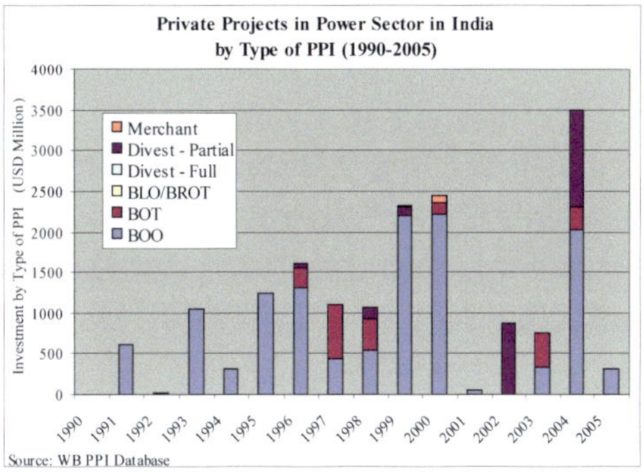

(d)

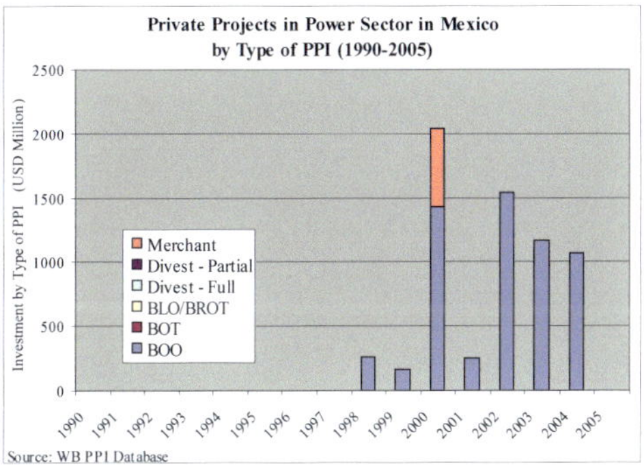

(e)

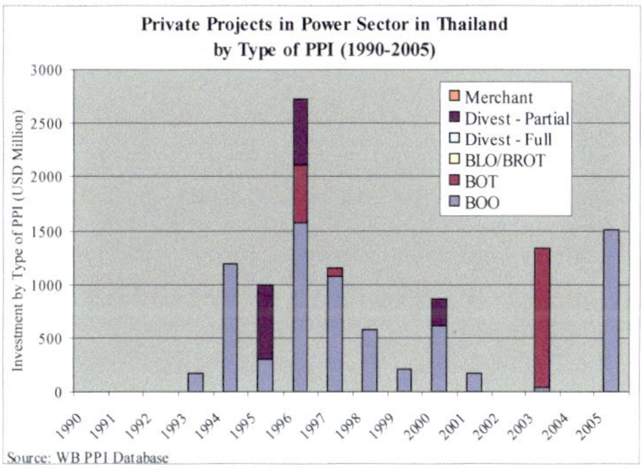

(f)

Fig. 9 Private Investment in the Power Sector by Mode of Participation

investors are able to assess risks associated with the merchant power plants. In Mexico, two BLT projects (a greenfield and a brownfield project) negotiated prior to enactment of IPP law in 1992 were later cancelled (NÚÑEZ-LUNA, 2005). In the case of Brazil, distribution privatisation was initiated in 1995 followed by divestiture of generation assets in 1997. As a competitive scenario evolved, investor owned merchant power plants were established few years later. While general conditions cited above did not exist in the Indian context, a small merchant hydro power plant was setup amidst power shortages and favourable economics of the project.

Private investment in Argentina and Brazil was dominated by divestiture of government assets. Due to domestic political compulsions, PRC, India, Mexico and Thailand adopted a more cautious approach and undertook limited sale of government owned utilities. The international investors who participate in the divestiture of public utilities in the crisis ridden countries became cautious of participating in privatisation programs. As a result, the privatisation of distribution companies in Delhi did not get enthusiastic response from investors, particularly the international investors. The energy crisis in California also affected acceptability of reforms and privatisation in developing countries. In these circumstances and the added domestic political compulsions led to shelving of privatisation of state distribution utilities in India[38].

[38] The proposed privatisation of the water utility in Delhi was also shelved under these circumstances.

12

Role of Multilateral Development Institutions

The improvement in infrastructure services has been emphasised for poverty reduction and socio-economic development in developing countries. With these objectives, multilateral development institutions (MDIs) like the World Bank, International Finance Corporation (IFC), Asian Development Bank (ADB), Inter American Development Bank (IADB), African Development Bank, European Bank for Reconstruction and Development (EBRD) have extended support to develop infrastructure projects in developing countries. Apart from supporting projects for capacity expansion and improving electricity access, these institutions play an important role in implementing reforms in the power sector.

During 1990-2005, the multilateral development institutions extended support to the electricity sector primarily through loans (USD 4.07 billion), loan syndication (USD 2.93 billion) and political risk guarantees (USD 2.31 billion) (Figs. 10-12). There was very limited participation through equity (USD 123.3 million) and risk management (USD 32.4 million). The overall support for the power sector in developing countries peaked in 2000 (USD 1.48 billion). The loan support peaked in 1998 (USD 527.2 million). This followed with greater emphasis on syndicated loans rather than direct loans to the sector.

The participation of Multilateral Development Institutions (MDIs) does not bring in substantial funds for the infrastructure sector including the power sector. However, their presence infuses confidence, and catalyses private and foreign investment in the sector in developing countries. The participation of MDIs brings a semblance of transparency and assures a competent due diligence of the project from socio-economic and political perspectives. The MDIs have been instrumental in bringing institutional reforms in the infrastructure sector in developing countries.

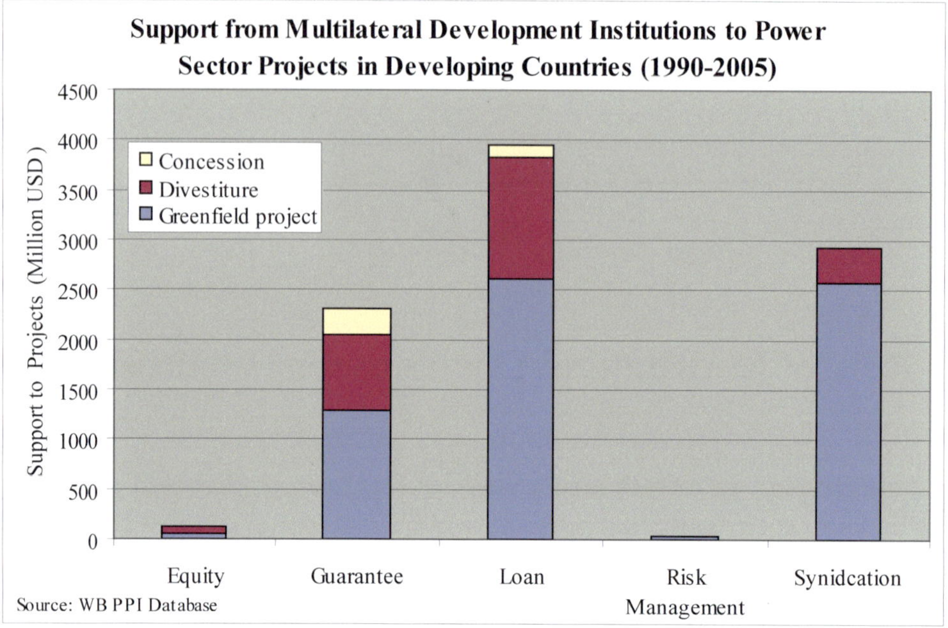

Fig. 10 Support from Multilateral Development Institutions to Power Sector Projects in Developing Countries (1990-2005)

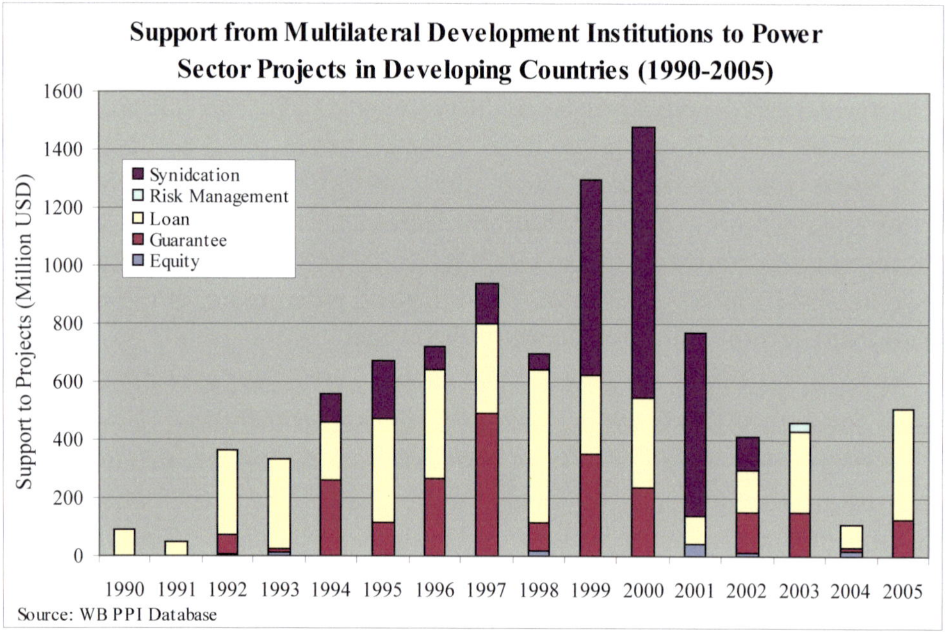

Fig. 11 Support from Multilateral Development Institutions to Power Sector Projects in Developing Countries (1990-2005)

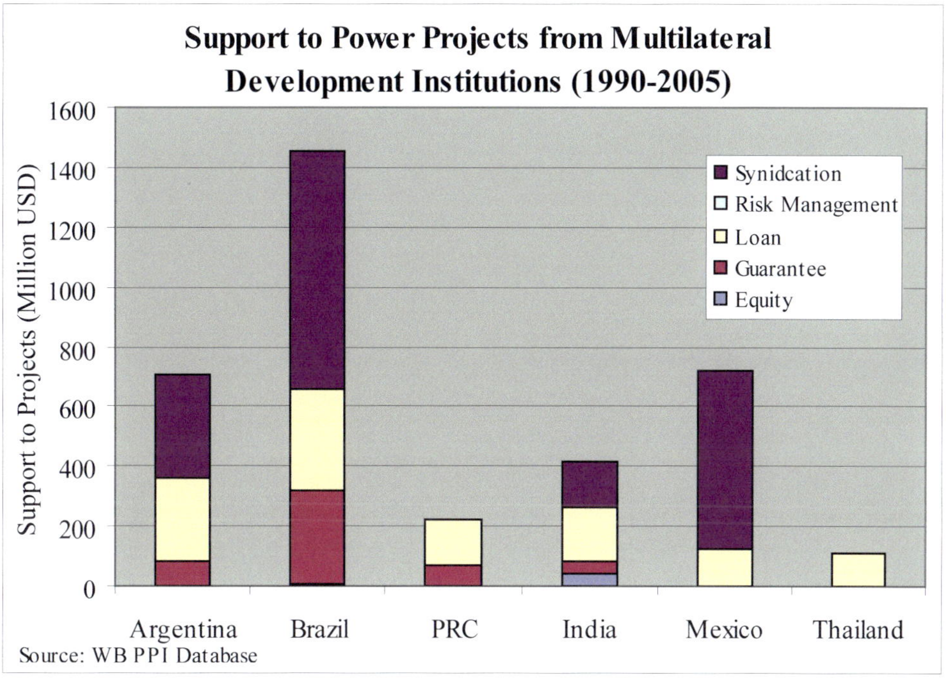

Fig. 12 Support from Multilateral Development Institutions to Power Sector Projects in Selected Countries (1990-2005)

The support from MDI is a drop in the ocean for the funds requirement for the power sector. Investment in the power sector in developing countries between 1990 and 2005 is estimated to be USD 261.32 billion, including USD 68.15 billion towards investment in government assets and USD193.17 billion in new facilities. The MDIs contribution towards the power sector in developing countries in the form of loans and loan syndication during the period totalled only USD7 billion. This represents about 2.68 % of the total investment in the sector. Considering the projected investment requirement of USD 5.1 trillion during 2000–30 (IEA, 2003a), the development institutions need to leverage higher investment into the sector. This would require not only an increase in the fund mobilisation by the MDIs but also require a re-look at their lending portfolio. Development institutions can derive a better mileage from their presence through political risk guarantees and loan syndication.

13

Projects under Distress and Investors' Sentiments

Power sector projects are characterised by long-term investment and are exposed to a variety of risks. Most of the commercial risks are addressed through contractual obligations like the power purchase agreement and the fuel supply agreement. A substantial change in the business environment or a failure to meet contractual obligations often leads to project distress, which may lead to project cancellation if the issues are not resolved to the satisfaction of parties involved. Macroeconomic crisis accentuated project distress with power projects in the East Asian and the Latin American countries.

Table 20

Cancelled and Distressed Power Sector Projects and Investment (1990 - 2004)

	Number of Projects	Investment (Million USD)
Argentina	21	9277.5
Brazil	2	3615.8
PRC	6	2889
India	3	2829.4
Mexico[39]	0	0
Thailand	0	0
Total (All countries in Database)	59	23663.7

Source: WB PPI Database accessed in Nov. 2005.

Infrastructure projects particularly those related to the independent power producers (IPPs) are prone to distress in developing countries as the business

[39] In Mexico, there were several cancelled projects based on flimsy legal foundations in 1990. A legal basis for operating IPPs was established in 1992.

and policy environment, and socio-political conditions are difficult to sustain over a long-term. A number of countries including, Argentina (21), Brazil (2) and PRC (6) have experienced troubled deals in the power sector (Table 20). India also has its share of the story more particularly due to the Dhabol controversy[40]. This seems to have obscured foreign investors' interest in the Indian power sector for some time and overshadowed a number of positive developments including liberalised policy and regulatory reforms.

Table 21
Regional Distribution of Electricity Projects under Stress (1984 - 2003)

Region	# of Projects	Value of Projects (USD million)	Percentage share of all Projects	Percentage share of investment in all Projects
East Asia and the Pacific	3	1,480.0	1	2
Europe and Central Asia	6	405.8	3	2
Latin America and the Caribbean	23	14,042.2	6	12
Middle East and North Africa	0	0	0	0
South Asia[41]	5	8,900.4	6	38
Sub-Saharan Africa	5	1,024.9	11	18
Total	42	25,853.3	4	10

Source: Covindassamy *et al.* (2005)

The distress of power sector projects, some of which are ultimately cancelled, can be attributed to a variety of reasons. Covindassamy *et al.* (2005) analyse 63 projects under stress in 18 countries (Table 21). Only 4% of the power projects are found to be under stress and a number of stressed projects are often rescued through renegotiation. Considering the value of investment under stress, the South Asian region did not seem to provide adequate comfort as a number of IPP deals in India and Pakistan were under a cloud (Table 21).

Covindassamy *et al.* (2005) find that pricing and regulatory issues inflict most of the stressed projects, followed by sociopolitical and macroeconomic issues respectively (Table 22). Further, it is found that the IPPs are less exposed to the distress risk than the privatized distribution companies. While IPPs hedge the

[40] The Dhabol power project was marred with controversy since the beginning due to alleged non-transparency and poor economics. A lopsided PPA raised many voices of concern over the economics of the projects (Sant *et al.*, 1995).

[41] This includes 22 stressed projects (with a total investment exposure of USD5.9 billion) in Pakistan. Covindassamy *et al.* (2005) considered these as a single project in their analysis.

Table 22
Cause of Power Project Under Stress

S. No.	Cause of Project Stress	Percentage of Projects Under Stress
1	Price-setting and Regulatory issues	90.3
2	Socio-political issues	73.8
3	Macroeconomic issues	71.4
4	Project structural problems	59.0
5	Poor Investors' performance	11.9

Source: Covindassamy *et al.* (2005)

market related risks through power purchase agreements (PPAs) with buyers, the distribution companies have less avenues to do so. Distribution companies are also exposed to greater regulatory risks and are more exposed to socio-political risks due to direct customer interface. Poor performance of the distribution companies and a higher degree of information asymmetry at the time of their divestiture accentuates risks to investors.

The PRC's enthusiasm to invite private and foreign investment in the power sector since the 1980s evaporated by the late 1990s on account of the increase in liquid capital in the country's financial system and the growing strength of state power companies. Foreign investors faced repeated tariff reductions and unenforceable contracts. This has been termed an example of 'obsolescing bargain'[42] (WOODHOUSE, 2005a). While such a situation may not lead to project distress in general, this dampens equity investors' enthusiasm and lenders' appetite for the sector.

Participation of the multilateral development institutions (MDIs) reduces distress related risk. This ensures a rigorous due diligence of the project by the participating MDI so as to ensure appropriate treatment of the risks[43]. This also encourages transparency in awarding projects and also helps in enlisting commitment by the host governments to undertake appropriate sectoral reforms. In the case of a project dispute arising out of an adverse socio-political situation or a policy reversal, the MDIs are in a position to exercise greater political leverage to avoid such situations.

[42] This was originally proposed by Vernon (1971) – as quoted in Woodhouse. It highlights shifting negotiating leverage between the host country and the investors during the project life cycle.

[43] In this context, it is interesting to note that the World Bank expressed serious reservations to the Dhabol power project in India and refused its participation in the same.

14

The Role of Public Investment and Domestic Capital

Liberalisation of investment environment in developing countries is primarily aimed at encouraging greater private and foreign investment in the sector. This led to reduction in public allocation of funds as well as reduction in resources earmarked by the multilateral agencies. Such resources play an important role to improve electricity access to rural and un-served areas. In the expectation of greater private investment, the Eighth (1992-1997) and the Ninth Five-Year (1997-2002) plans of India included a sharp reduction in plan allocation in proportion to the total plan outlay (Fig. 13). A not-so-encouraging response from private investors led to its enhancement in the Tenth Five-Year plan (2002-07). The proportion of plan allocation for the power sector has consequently risen to 18.2 % for current plan (GOI, 2002b).

The growing investment requirement[44] in the power sector places demand for investors equity capital as well as a debt funds. The investments in the sector are highly leveraged[45] and also require long-term loans. The prudential sectoral exposure norms, prescribed by the banking regulator, limit the exposure of the banks and financial institutions to the sector. The longer tenure requirement for lending to the sector also limits availability of suitable funds. The appetite for long-term debt instruments in the domestic market is also limited. The domestic bond market in the country is dominated by government borrowing leaving limited space for the private sector.

Borrowing in foreign currency is attractive on account of lower cost of interest. This, however, exposes the project and hence the tariffs to exchange rate fluctuations. The established Indian companies have successfully raised for-

[44] Investment requirement projected by the Kohli Committee for the Xth and XIth five-year plan are given in Appendix B.

[45] The regulatory benchmark for debt-to-equity ratio is 70:30. However, a high leverage up to 80:20 is being proposed for a number of new projects including the Ultra Mega Power Projects.

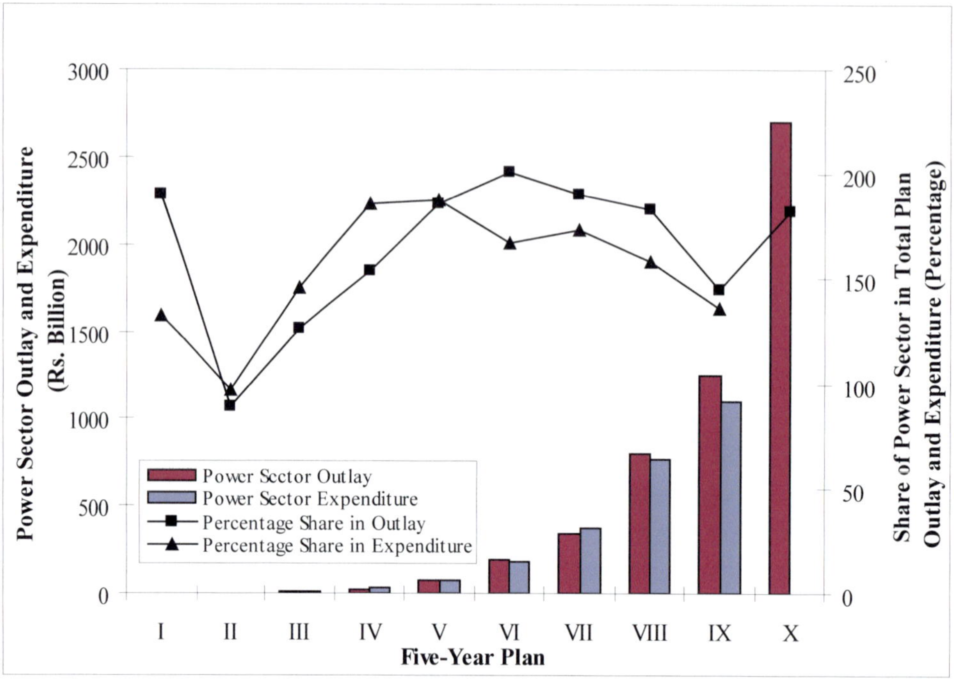

Fig. 13 Trend in Plan Outlay for the Indian Power Sector

eign currency denominated debt from international markets. This is, however, governed by the regulations related to external commercial borrowings (ECBs). These regulations limit ECB through automatic route up to USD 20 million for minimum average maturity of three years and up to USD 500 million with minimum average maturity of five years. As per the recent credit policy announced in October 2006, an additional amount of USD 250 million for average minimum maturity of ten years can be raised under the approval route.

A softening of the domestic interest rate as compared to the last decade and the concerns about fluctuations in exchange rate, have renewed focus on domestic borrowing. The Indian debt market, however, remains dominated by public borrowing, which accounts for 96.02% of the total domestic market borrowings (Table 23). Private financial institutions and corporate entities constitute just 3.98% of the capital mop up from the domestic debt market. In contrast to this, private financial institutions and corporate entities account for 42.78%, 65.42% and 74.53% of the domestic borrowing in PRC, Thailand and S. Korea respectively. Limited access to capital markets and high transaction costs impede expansion of the corporate bond market. This makes it desirable to undertake financial sector reforms alongside or before the initiation of reforms in the power sector, where a greater role for private investors is envisaged. A mature capital market also facilitates project developers to raise long-term debt in domestic capital markets.

Table 23
Domestic Debt Securities in Emerging Economies (June 2006)

	Public	Private FIs	Corporate Entities	Total	Public	Private FIs	Corporate Entities	Total
	Billion USD				Percentage Share			
All Issuers	21618.5	17546.4	5149.7	44314.6	48.78	39.60	11.62	100
Argentina	41.6	5.0	10.8	57.4	72.47	8.71	18.82	100
Brazil	409.5	108.4	4.8	522.6	78.36	20.74	0.92	100
PRC	340.3	252.5	12.5	605.3	56.22	41.71	2.07	100
India	268.00	7.30	3.80	279.10	96.02	2.62	1.36	100
Mexico	186.50	6.40	34.80	227.80	81.87	2.81	15.28	100
S. Korea	38.00	16.30	24.70	79.00	48.10	20.63	31.27	100
Thailand	226.00	277.00	152.60	656.70	34.41	42.18	23.24	100

Source: BIS (2006)

Project financing of power projects requires long-tenure lending with a moratorium until the completion of the construction phase. The project financing market has taken off in India as a number of infrastructure projects are financed in this manner. The domestic financial institutions provide various financial solutions including take-out financing once the construction phase for a project is completed. In mature markets, power projects financed through the project financing route also garner funds through long-term bond markets[46]. The domestic bond market has not attained maturity to absorb long-term instruments for power projects with an economic life of about 20–25 years. Municipal bonds for tenures up to seven years have been utilised to raise funds by municipal bodies. This has been supported by 'negotiated ratings' i.e. the clients undertake certain reforms steps to reduce losses and provide multiple security cover through escrow accounts, till an acceptable level of rating is achieved. These bonds are thinly traded and investors face an illiquid secondary market. The domestic bond market is yet to mature and provide adequate resources of desirable tenure for the power sector.

In order to attract private investment, governments offer support to investors, often in the form of grants, soft loans or guarantees. An increasing number of governments have developed an institutional approach to support funding

[46] Financial solutions like take-out financing are provided buy the domestic financial institutions in India. In the recent past, a hydro power project developer successfully raised equity finance through an IPO once the project entered the operation phase.

in domestic markets. Such institutions leverage government and donor funding, reduce transaction costs for smaller-scale infrastructure financings, increase transparency and maintain consistency in evaluating and allocating government support and facilitate portfolio diversification (KLINGEBIEL and RUSTER, 2000).

The weakness of local capital markets in most developing countries impedes investment in infrastructure sector (WORLD BANK, 2004). The domestic banking sector in developing countries is often unable to meet the demand for long-term funds for infrastructure sector. Development of the domestic capital markets and encouragement of contractual saving through pension, provident funds and insurance markets can help address the long-term financial requirement of the sector (KUMAR *et al.*, 1997; WB/USAID, 2004.).

The exposure norms for the banks and FIs limit their exposure to the a single borrower or a business group[47]. In the case of large infrastructure projects these limits could be easily reached. Relaxation of such regulatory provisions by the Reserve Bank of India can provide more funds for the infrastructure including the power sector. This is, however, guided by the regulatory prudence to ensure health of the financial sector in general. The larger issue of asset-liability mismatch hinders the ability of the banks and financial institutions to lend funds for a long-term. The Kohli Committee on financing of power sector for the Xth and XIth five-year plan suggested a number of measures to bolster availability of funds, more specifically domestic debt, for the power sector (GOI, 1998). These include provision of priority sector status for lending to the power sector by banks and financial institutions, and tax exemptions to power sector specific funds. Domestic financial institutions are allowed to raise funds for infrastructure lending through tax free bonds. An increase in the limit of qualified investment in these bonds would help garner larger funds for the sector. Extension of tax benefits for subscription to such investments would help channalise greater domestic savings, which otherwise seek short-term debt instruments. The Task Force on Power Sector Investment and Reform recommended rationalisation of the prevailing fiscal regime (GOI, 2004).

The domestic banks and financial institutions (FIs) can leverage their core competence of project appraisal and adopt a number of strategies to expand deployment of available funds. Loan syndication provides for pooling of resources by a number of FIs for large projects. The FIs can also securitise the loans, fully or partially, once the project has begun commercial operation (JAIN, 1998). This will require reforms in the domestic debt market for development of an active

[47] Credit exposure norms for banks and FIs limit their exposure to a business group up to 40% of their capital funds. In the case of a single borrower this is limited to 15% of the bank's/FI's capital.

and liquid market for securitised loans. Investment in such securitised bonds can be extended tax benefits similar to those available to infrastructure bonds floated by the FIs. Under similar benefits, open-ended sector-specific mutual funds will also help garner equity as well as debt funds for the power sector.

Governments in many countries have devised an institutional approach to support funding infrastructure projects. These institutions have, however, failed to deliver desired results in many countries. From a study of five case studies in developing countries, KLINGEBIEL and RUSTER (2000) identify two main sets of reasons for failure of such institutions to fall short of their objective to support infrastructure investment - absence of a conducive environment for private participation in infrastructure; and fault in the facility design. The authors find that environment for private participation in infrastructure was not conducive due to poor sector policies, an unstable macroeconomic environment, and inadequate financial sector policies. The problems related to the project design were primarily in terms of the sectors targeted, pricing of instruments, and consistency of objectives and instruments.

15

Policy Recommendations

Power shortages, lagging public investment and poor performance of state utilities translated into a need to attract private participation in the power sector in developing countries. This was facilitated, often under the guidance of multilateral development agencies, by reforms and restructuring in the sector. Various countries have followed a differing path and pace to such a reform process. This included introduction of policies to permit private investment in the sector, partial or full divestiture of public assets, setting up of independent regulatory institutions and power market development. The outcome of such a process also varies across countries. The literature review and the comparative policy analysis among the selected Asian and Latin American countries enable us to make the following recommendations for policy intervention and regulatory action for encouraging private investment. While these are spelled out in the context of the Indian power sector, most of these are equally applicable in the context of developing countries which exhibit similar characteristics in terms of the socio-economic conditions and the state of the power sector.

15.1 Macroeconomic Stability and Fiscal Management

Macroeconomic instability leading to a fall in the exchange rate is one of the most prominent causes of project stress worldwide. Stable macroeconomic environment particularly helps foreign investment in the power sector. Due to non-exportable nature of electricity[48], forex risk management through financing engineering needs to be emphasised not only for the project developer but also for the buyer utilities who assume this risk in the case of pass through costs. Adept management of exchange rate by the Indian central bank, the Reserve Bank

[48] Limited electricity trade with Nepal (net export) and Bhutan (net import) is denominated in the Indian currency.

of India, and comfortable forex reserve position has allayed fears of macroeconomic instability for investors (FICI, 2003). Structuring power projects with significant domestic private sector equity financing and debts in the local currency can significantly lower their exposure to such risks. Additional concerns arise due to domestic inflation especially when project developers are not able to pass through this risk to buyers. This not only affects the cost of power produced but also exposes the lenders if interest rates do not assume the inflationary impact. In this context, fiscal management by the government plays an important role in development of domestic debt market. The enactment of the Fiscal Responsibility and Budget Management Act 2003 has put in place a commitment of the government towards maintaining a fiscal discipline. However, there are concerns due to need for fiscal prudence by the states and non-targeted subsidies.

15.2 Policy Stability and Reduction in Regulatory Uncertainty

Uncertainty is universally disliked by investors. An approach for encouraging private investment in the power sector should focus on reducing risks itself rather than allocating it (Malhotra, 1997). This would increase the number of bankable projects, which are rather lacking in developing countries like India. While commercial risk remains a part of usual business endeavour, policy and regulatory risk is best addressed through transparent and predictable policies and regulations. A roadmap to the process of reforms and a multi-year regulatory framework at the state level can help to reduce these risks. The central as well as state governments provide various fiscal and other incentives for private investment in the sector, the uncertainty associated with their scope and continuity fails to enlist investors' commitment for long-term projects. A piecemeal approach to reforms generally dilutes the interest of the investors, who need to secure lender's commitment for long-term funds on the basis of transparent and stable policies. India has a positive legacy of a strong legal system. However, concern for policy reversals looms large in an political regime. This deters investors, more particularly the foreign investors, to venture into jurisdictions characterised by political instability.

The independence of regulatory institutions is another concern for investors. A lack of independence may overshadow a tariff rationalisation program due to its potential political repercussions and also influences regulatory certainty often under the influence of a changing political regime. This limits the licensees' ability to recover their costs and earn a reasonable rate of return. The National Electricity Policy (NEP) stresses the need for regulatory certainty through independent regulation (GOI, 2005a).

"... the need for regulatory certainty based on independence of the regulatory commissions and transparency in their functioning to generate investor's confidence."

Such policy statements need to be translated into a political resolve to distance the government from selection process of regulators and to provide financial independence to the regulatory institutions.

Investors in privatised distribution utilities are exposed to a regulatory risk if a medium-term road map to performance standards and tariffs can not be committed under the prevailing regulatory regime. The adoption of a multi-year tariff framework will provide some comfort to investors and will also ensure a better response to future divestiture of state owned distribution utilities. Distribution reforms, targeted to improve the performance of distribution utilities, also alleviate the risk perception of investors. Strengthening of the Accelerated Power Development and Reforms Programme (APDRP) with a milestone based disbursement and contracting reforms to ensure efficient utilisation of funds would help in this direction.

The ongoing reform process aims at ushering in greater competition in the power sector. A road map to development of power markets including exchange based spot and futures trading is yet to emerge. This helps investors, especially in the merchant power plants, to chalk out an investment strategy for the sector. The un-liberalised coal market continues to place stress on fuel supply even as the existing plants faced supply shortages in not-so-distant past. The unfinished liberalisation of the coal sector needs to be addressed earnestly. This not only holds up investment for development of the coal market, but also hinders investment in the power sector. A time consuming and non-transparent process for seeking allocation of domestic coal blocks for thermal power plants frustrates the investor sentiments.

15.3 Performance of Distribution Utilities

The poor financial and operational performance of distribution utilities remains a key concern for investors in power generation. Phased open access regime for direct sale to customers is not expected to provide substantial market for new generation assets immediately due to cross-subsidy surcharge. A significant part of demand growth is expected to come within the network of distribution utilities, which remain the key customers for IPPs. From the recent experience, it is evident that privatisation of distribution utilities remains unattractive to investors and desires a lot of a political courage.

Due to a lack of regulatory independence, the political economy of electricity prices remains a key concern. Investors are unlikely to be interested if they are unable to generate sufficient cash flows due to low tariffs and payment risks. Timing and sequencing of privatisation, a perceived panacea for all the ills of the public sector, is critical to the success of privatisation itself and the reforms program (Rosenzweig and Voll, 1997). If existing state utilities are able to reduce technical and financial losses, and improve recoveries, a privatisation program would be more attractive to investors. This would also help to achieve the ultimate goal of a reduction in shortages through investment and an improvement in efficiency in the sector in the long-run. ADB (2000) recommends that regulators should prepare the distribution utilities for privatisation by reduction in subsidies and cross-subsidies. Early privatisation of the poorly performing distribution utilities, without ample commercial space, may not lead to speedy recovery. This makes the process of turnaround less popular and slows down privatisation effort in other states. Greater commercial autonomy with adequate incentive structure and independence from political interference are desirable to improve the health of the distribution segment. One may argue that a turnaround of corporatised distribution utilities could obviate the need for privatisation. However, the risk of falling back into an inefficiency trap and the fear of political interventions would continue to linger under the public ownership. This would require turning back to increased subsidies, taking resources away from other social sectors that require the government's attention. As evident from the experience in Orissa and Delhi, privatisation may not be a panacea to all the ills of the power sector as it is not immune to political interventionism and regulatory uncertainty. Unless these issues are addressed, a privatisation exercise in future may not find many takers from the private sector.

As mentioned above, a poor state of distribution utilities discourages investment by the IPPs. Further, a lack of counter guarantees and limited escrowability of distribution utilities requires urgent attention to improve the cash flow. This would mean that tariffs would need to be rationalised, i.e. increased, for subsidised categories. The political system cannot hope to keep the high ground on subsidised tariffs for a large political base and also try to fill the widening power supply gap through enhanced private and sustainable public investment. Phased direct access to large consumers also highlights the urgency to improve the operational efficiency and financial performance of state utilities. This may result in loss of lucrative customers, which traditionally cross-subsidise other politically sensitive consumer categories and hence further aggravate the financial situation.

The privatised distribution utilities are currently outside the purview of the APDRP. Their inclusion in the APDRP's incentive scheme would help enlist larger participation in the privatisation programs in future. In such a case, the incentive to improve performance would be significant as these distribution utilities will also get incentives for reduction in cash losses. This would, however, shift the burden of financial assistance from the state to the central government[49]. In doing so, the central government will provide incentive for greater private participation in the weak distribution utilities and will also assist their speedy recovery. This should not result in additional budgetary support as the incentive for performance improvement would have been extended in any case to the state owned distribution utilities. While such costs would be borne by the central government, the state government would gain in terms of increased valuation of distribution utilities and/or reduced subsidy support.

15.4 Foreign Investment as Joint Ventures with Domestic Partners

Information asymmetry and market knowledge makes its desirable for foreign investors to rope in domestic partners. The open access regime accentuates the advantages of local market knowledge. At an associate to foreign partner, domestic partners provide local expertise in negotiating contracts in a multi-buyer system and negotiating with the political process.

Given the existing investment framework in India, there are additional advantages to foreign investors associating as joint partner with the CPSUs such as NTPC, NHPC and PGCIL. The key financial implication of such minority joint ventures is that it provides a market access to CPSUs on non-competitive basis for the next five years and assures a 14 % return on equity apart from incentives beyond benchmarks[50]. The other important factor is the avoidance of payment risk from the state distribution utilities. The CPSUs have been assured payment security as per a tripartite agreement that led to the settlement of dues of the erstwhile SEBs. In case of payment default, these central sector utilities have access to the funds earmarked from the central plan allocation to the respective state governments (GOI, 2001).

Direct access to customers brings a ray of hope for private investors. The choice is between entering into a single contract with an insolvent single-buyer state distribution utility and dealing with a number of large industrial and commercial consumers with much less payment risk. The knowledge of the local market conditions and the political climate would provide an edge to domestic private investors over the foreign ones.

The participation of foreign partners not only brings in foreign equity, but also improves access to international finance on back of their experience and

[49] In the case of the privatisation program for the distribution utilities in Delhi, the state government committed a financial support of USD720 million over a period of five years.

[50] Refer to Section 6 for details.

greater domain knowledge. The presence of a strong local partner would avoid project distress, especially that arising out of a political risk. It would also help a speedy dispute resolution and would streamline the renegotiation process, in case necessary.

15.5 Develop Project and Regulatory Templates for Rural Electrification

An improvement in the investment climate for small private providers of infrastructure services can help increase access to these services especially in rural and isolated areas (World Bank, 2005a). The Electricity Act 2003 has opened up avenues for small entrepreneurs, who can build independent grids to serve licensee free rural areas or become franchise of a distribution licensee. While some of these projects may be economically viable, they face scale disadvantage in terms of their ability to raise long-term debt as well as to reduce project development cost. Domestic financial institutions like the Rural Electrification Corporation (REC) can extend a long-term debt to projects meeting certain technical and regulatory norms. Such institutions can also channelise long-term funds from contractual savings i.e. insurance and pension funds.

Since a number of stand alone projects may utilise renewable energy including small-hydro and biomass based hybrid systems, the role of government agencies promoting renewable energy also needs to be streamlined to reduce transaction costs. Development of project templates for a variety of technological options would help reduce project development cost. These should also include a sub-module for a project development document to harness benefits from CDM credits for such for small projects. This will improve the financial viability of projects utilising renewable energy sources. The project templates are to be developed in coordination with the SERCs, who also need to develop appropriate regulatory templates prescribing operational and financial parameters including tariffs. This would reduce regulatory uncertainty for investors in such small scale projects.

15.6 Enhanced Commitment from Multilateral Development Institutions

Credit enhancement mechanism are often necessary to assure debt financing for infrastructure projects especially during the transition period till domestic capital markets deepen sufficiently. These mechanisms may include targeted guarantees, partial subsidies or direct participation in the projects (Kumar *et al.*, 1997). Multilateral institutions play a significant role in such credit enhancement mechanisms for infrastructure sector. The participation of multilateral institutions like the World Bank and the ADB promotes investors' confidence and leverages investment in the sector. This also helps to reduce risk for lenders, who continue to bank on the due diligence of such institutions. A further expansion of risk management facilities for investment in the power sector would also add to investor confidence.

A higher social rate of return on infrastructure investments (CANNING and BENNATHAN, 2000), especially in rural electrification and rural road and transport services would continue to demand investment support from the government and multilateral institutions. Such support should be limited to facilitating project development and financing viability gap determined in a competitive manner. However, the efficiency of public investment in such schemes needs to be scrutinized and wherever feasible, private participation should be encouraged to achieve long-term goal-oriented outcomes.

16

Conclusions

The electricity supply has been in the public domain in most of the developing countries. Under public ownership, the sector is not been able to catch up with the growing demand for electricity. The operational inefficiency and financial losses often lead to poor quality of supply and underinvestment. A wave of reforms has swept through a number of developing countries. These reforms were primarily targeted to improve the performance of the state owned companies and to provide a conducive atmosphere for private investment in the sector.

The erstwhile vertically integrated SEBs in India have been riddled with inefficiencies due to a lack of accountability and administrative bottlenecks. Reforms in the Indian power sector were initiated to restructure the SEBs and to set up independent regulatory institutions. The Electricity Act 2003 led to deepening of the reform process by enabling competition in wholesale electricity market and retail electricity supply, in phases. Thirteen SEBs have so far unbundled into separate generation, transmission and distribution companies. Beginning with the establishment of an independent regulatory commission in Orissa in 1996, the SERCs have been set up in all states. Some of the smaller states in the North East have established a Joint Electricity Regulatory Commission. The process of tariff determination has become more transparent and limited tariff rationalisation has been undertaken against consumer opposition and political meddling.

The emerging competition in the bulk power market and phased direct access to large consumers is aimed at reducing the risks associated with sales to financially weak state utilities. The policy and regulatory developments are promising, but more needs to be done to improve the performance of distribution utilities. Amongst other factors, the autonomy to manage these utilities in a commercial manner remains a key issue. In the long-run, the state's objectives are best served by nurturing a financially sustainable sector that can improve access for poor and rural consumers.

This research undertook a review of the policy and regulatory developments in the Indian power sector. A review of the literature and a comparative policy analysis helped us to unravel some of the lessons to be learned for the process of reform in developing countries in general. The initial phase of power sector reform in India allowed commercially-oriented IPPs to sell power to financially weak SEBs, which do not rely on sound commercial principles. This marriage of convenience is not sustainable. The initial phase of reforms in developing countries should be aimed to restructure the sector and to set up an independent regulator. As private participation grows, it would be suitable to introduce competition in the sector. This would not only help lower the cost of power purchase, it would also provide greater incentive for performance improvement. The experience of private sector investment in Latin American countries relied on the introduction of commercial interest in the bulk power market by inviting IPPs as well as introducing commercial principles at the end of buyer utilities through their divestiture.

The experience in East Asia and Latin America suggests that macroeconomic stability remains a key to attracting sustainable and increased investment in the infrastructure sectors. India continues to demonstrate macroeconomic stability along with prudent currency management. Future growth prospects in the power sector hold substantial potential for private investment. However, the financial performance of the state owned distribution utilities remains a key concern for investors. A positive outcome of existing distribution privatisation programs would guide such future plans, which remain politically sensitive. The regulatory challenge is to provide incentives for improvement in technical efficiency and financial performance.

The unavailability of sovereign guarantees can be adequately addressed if state utilities become viable through greater commercialisation, if not privatisation. Inability of the domestic capital market to provide long-term debt for the power sector needs to be adequately addressed by encouraging contractual saving through life insurance and pension funds, and channelising these for the power sector. Securitisation of project loans after the construction period and development of secondary bond market would help garner funds for investment in the sector.

The long-term interest of the consumers can only be served if reasonably priced electricity is available over the long-run. Political interests would best be served by depoliticising tariffs, which would be beneficial to consumers in the long-term through improved quality and reliability of supply. Given the objective to electrify all villages by 2010 and to double the generating capacity in the country by 2012, the need to improving policy environment and strengthening regulatory framework can not be undermined.

References

ADB, JBIC & WB (2005), *Connecting East Asia: A New Framework for Infrastructure*, Asian Development Bank, Japan Bank For International Cooperation and The World Bank, Washington, DC.

ADB (2000), *Developing Best Practices for Promoting Private Sector Investment in Infrastructure: Power*, Asian Development Bank, Manila.

BIS (2006), BIS Quarterly Review June 2006, Bank for International Settlements, Zurich, Downloaded from http://www.bis.org/publ/qtrpdf/r_qa0606.pdf in June 2006.

BLACKMAN, Allen and WU, Xun (1999), "Foreign direct investment in China's power sector: trends, benefits and barriers", *Energy Policy*, 27, 695-711.

BRICENO, C., ESTACHE, A. and SHAFIK, N. (2004), "Infrastructure Services In Developing Countries: Access, Quality, Costs and Policy Reform", World Bank Policy Research Working Paper 3468, The World Bank, Washington, DC.

CEA (2006a), *General Review 2006*, Central Electricity Authority, New Delhi.

CEA (2006b). "Monthly Review of Power Sector - March 2006." Central Electricity Authority, New Delhi downloaded from http://cea.nic.in in April 2006.

CEA (2005a), *General Review 2005*, Central Electricity Authority, New Delhi.

CEA (2005b), Monthly Review of Power Sector (Executive Summary) December 2005, downloaded from http://cea.nic.in/power_sec_reports/executive_summary/2005_12/24-30.pdf

CEA (2001), *Sixteenth Electric Power Survey of India*, Central Electricity Authority, New Delhi.

CEE (2006), "Results of Electricity Sector Restructuring in Argentina", Case Study from New Era in Oil, Gas and Power Value Creation, Center for Energy Economics (CEE), Bureau of Economic Geology, The University of Texas at Austin, Houston, TX. Accessed from http://www.beg.utexas.edu/energyecon/new-era/ in June 2006.

CERC (2004), Terms and Conditions of Tariff Regulations 2004, Central Electricity Regulatory Commission, New Delhi.

CERC (2000), Terms and Conditions of Tariff, Central Electricity Regulatory Commission, New Delhi.

CALDERÓN, César and SERVÉN, Luis (2004), "The Effects of Infrastructure Development on Growth and income Distribution", Working Papers No. 270, Central Bank of Chile, Huérfanos.

CANNING, David and PEDRONI, Peter (2004), "The Effect of Infrastructure on Long Run Economic Growth", Accessed from http://www.williams.edu/Economics/wp/pedroniinfrastructure.pdf in Oct. 2005.

CANNING, David and BENNATHAN, Esra (2000), "The Social Rate of Return on Infrastructure Investments", Working Paper # 2390, Queen's University at Belfast Northern Ireland, U.K. a part of a World Bank research project "Infrastructure and Growth: A Multicountry Panel Study" (RPO 680-89).

COVINDASSAMY, M. A., ODA, D and ZHANG, Y. (2005), "Analysis of Power Projects with Private Participation under Stress", Energy Sector Management Assistance Program, The World Bank, Washington, DC.

CRISIL/ICRA (2006), State Power Sector Performance Ratings: Final Report to the Ministry of Power, downloaded from http://powermin.nic.in in Sept. 2006

CRISIL/ICRA (2005), Power Sector Rating Consolidated Report to the Ministry of Power, Accessed from http://powermin.nic.in in Sept. 2005

CRISIL/ICRA (2004), Power Sector Rating Consolidated Report to the Ministry of Power (Revised), Accessed from http://powermin.nic.in in Sept. 2005

CRISIL/ICRA (2003), Report on Rating of State Power Sectors, Accessed from http://powermin.nic.in in Sept. 2005

CROW, Robert T. (2001), "Foreign Direct Investment in New Electricity Generating Capacity in Developing Asia: Stakeholders, Risks, and the Search for a New Paradigm", Asia/Pacific Research Center, Stanford University, Stanford, CA.

DAILAMI, Monsoor and KLEIN, Michael (1997), "Government Support to Private Infrastructure Projects in Emerging Markets", in Irwin, T., Klein, M., Perry, G. E. and Thobani, M. (eds.) (1997), "Dealing with Public Risk in Private Infrastructure", The World Bank, Washington, DC.

DFID (2002), "Making Connections: Infrastructure for Poverty Reduction," Department for International Development, London.

DUNNING, J.H. (1993), *Multinational Enterprises and the Global Economy*, Addison-Wesley, Wokingham.

ESTACHE, Antonio (2004), "Emerging infrastructure policy issues in developing countries - a survey of the recent economic literature" Background Paper for the October 2004 Berlin meeting of the POVNET Infrastructure Working Group, The World Bank, Washington, DC.

ESTACHE, Antonio and GOICOECHEA, Ana (2005), "How widespread were private investment and regulatory reform in infrastructure utilities during the 1990s?" World Bank Policy Research Working Paper # 3595, The World Bank, Washington, DC.

ESTACHE, Antonio and PINGLO, Maria Elena, (2004), "Are Returns to Private Infrastructure in Developing Countries Consistent with Risks Since the Asian Crisis?" World Bank Policy Research Working Paper # 3373, The World Bank, Washington, DC.

FAY, M. and YEPES, T. (2003), "Investing in Infrastructure: What is needed from 2000-2010", World Bank, Policy Research Working Paper No. 3102, The World Bank, Washington, DC.

FICCI (2003), FDI Survey 2003, Federation of Indian Chambers of Commerce & Industry, New Delhi.

FICCI (2002), FDI Survey 2002, Federation of Indian Chambers of Commerce & Industry, New Delhi.

GLOBERMAN, Steven and SHAPIRO, Daniel (2002), Global Foreign Direct Investment Flows: The Role of Governance Infrastructure, *World Development,* 30 (11) 1899–1919.

GOI (2006), National Tariff Policy, Ministry of Power, Government of India, New Delhi.

GOI (2005a), National Electricity Policy, Ministry of Power, Government of India, New Delhi.

GOI (2005b), Mid-Term Appraisal of the Tenth Five Year Plan (2002-07), Planning Commission, Government of India, New Delhi.

GOI (2005c), Widening Scope for Private Participation, Ministry of Power, Government of India, New Delhi.

GOI (2002a), Kohli Committee on Financing of Power Sector During X and XI Plan, Planning Commission, Government of India, New Delhi.

GOI (2002b), Tenth Five Year Plan (2002-07), Planning Commission, Government of India, New Delhi.

GOI (2001), Report of the Expert Group Settlement of SEB Dues, Planning Commission, Government of India, New Delhi.

GOI (1996), *The India Infrastructure Report*, Ministry of Finance, Government of India, New Delhi.

HENISZ, Witold J (2002), The institutional environment for infrastructure investment, *Industrial and Corporate Change,* 11 (2), 355 – 389.IEA (2003a), World Energy Investment Outlook. International Energy Agency, Paris.

IEA (2003b), Power Generation Investment in Liberalised Electricity Markets, Discussion Paper, International Energy Agency, Paris.

IIE (2002), "Best Practices Guide: Electricity Regulation in Latin America", The Energy Group, Institute for International Education, Washington DC. Accessed from http://www.iie.org in Oct. 2005.

JAIN, R. K. (1998), "Financing of Power Projects in India: Problems and Prospects - A Note", Occasional Papers, Reserve Bank of India, Mumbai.

IRWIN, T., KLEIN, M., PERRY, G. E. and THOBANI, M. (eds.) (1997), "Dealing with Public Risk in Private Infrastructure", The World Bank, Washington, DC.

IZAGUIRRE, Ada Karina (2005), "Private Infrastructure", Public Policy for the Private Sector, Note No. 299, The World Bank, Washington, DC.

KIRKPATRICK, C, PARKER, D and ZHANG, Y (2004), "Foreign Direct Investment in Infrastructure in Developing Countries: Does Regulation Make A Difference?" Presented at the Asian Development Bank Institute (ADBI) Annual Conference on 'Infrastructure and Development: Poverty, Regulation and Private Sector Development', Tokyo, 6th December 2004.

KLINGEBIEL, Daniela and RUSTER, Jeff (2000), "Why Infrastructure Often Fall Short of Their Objectives", World Bank Policy Research Working Paper # 2358, The World Bank, Washington, DC.

KUMAR, A., GRAY, R. D., HOSHKOTE, M., KLAUDY, S., and RUSTER, J. (1997), "Mobilizing Domestic Capital Markets for Infrastructure Financing-International Experiences and Lessons for China", World Bank Working Discussion Paper # 377, The World Bank, Washington, DC.

LAMB, Peter M. (2005), "The Indian Electricity Market: Country Study and Investment Context", Working Paper # 48, Program on Energy and Sustainable Development at Stanford University, Stanford.

LAMECH, Ranjit and SAEED, Kazim (2003), "What International Investors Look for When Investing in Developing Countries: Results from a Survey of International Investors in the Power Sector", Energy and Mining Sector Board Discussion Paper # 6, The World Bank, Washington, DC.

MALHOTRA, Anil K (1997), Private Participation in Infrastructure - Lessons from Asia's Power Sector, *Finance & Development*, December, 33 - 35.

MILLAN, J., LORA, E., and MICCO, A. (2001), Sustainability of the Electricity Sector Reforms in Latin America, Seminar on "Towards Competitiveness: The Institutional Path", Annual Meetings of the Board of Governors, Inter-American Development Bank and Inter-American Investment Corporation, March 16, Santiago, Chile.

MORAN, T. (1999), "Foreign Direct Investment and Development", Institute for International Economics, Washington DC.

NERA (1998), Governance and Regulatory Regimes for Private Sector Infrastructure Development, TAS No. 5758, A Report for the ADB, National Economic Research Associates, London.

NSE (2006), Shareholding Pattern of Various Companies. National Stock Exchange, Mumbai. Downloaded from www.nseindia.com in April 2006.

NÚÑEZ-LUNA, Alejandra (2005), "Private Power Production in Mexico - A Country Study", Working Paper # 47, Program on Energy and Sustainable Development, Center for Environmental Science and Policy, Stanford University, Stanford, CA.

NÚÑEZ-LUNA, Alejandra and WOODHOUSE, Erik J. (2005), "The IPP Investment Experience in Argentina", Working Paper # 44, Program on Energy and Sustainable Development, Center for Environmental Science and Policy, Stanford University, Stanford, CA.

OLIVEIRA, Adilson de (2003), "The Political Economy of the Brazilian Power Industry Reform", Working Paper # 2, Program on Energy and Sustainable Development, Center for Environmental Science and Policy, Stanford University, Stanford, CA.

PARGAL, Sheoli (2003), "Regulation and Private Sector Investment in Infrastructure Evidence from Latin America", Policy Research Working Paper # 3037, The World Bank, Washington, DC.

PROTEGO (2000), "El Rol de la Banca y de la Iniciativa Privada en el Desarrollo de Proyectos de Energía en México", III Congreso Nacional AMEE, 25 May 2000, As quoted in Núñez-Luna (2005).

Rosenzweig, M. B., Pabon-Agudelo, C., Voll, Sarah P. & Neto, Jose Simoes (2001), Power Sector Reform in Brazil: Challenges to Private Investment, National Economic Research Associates, Washington DC.

Rosenzweig, M. B. & Voll, Sarah P. (1997), Sequencing Power Sector Privatization - Is Reform Its Precondition or Result?, National Economic Research Associates, Washington DC.

Sader, Frank (1999), "Attracting Foreign Direct Investment into Infrastructure: Why is it so Difficult?", The World Bank, Washington DC.

Sant, Girish, Dixit, Shantanu and Wagle, Subodh (1995), "The Power Purchase Agreement (PPA) Between Dabhol Power Company and Maharashtra State Electricity Board: The Structure and its Techno-Economic Implications", *Economic and Political Weekly*, June.

Singh, Anoop (2006), "Power Sector Reform in India: Current Issues and Prospects", *Energy Policy*, 34(16) 2480-2490.

Sirtaine, Sophie, Pinglo, Maria Elena, Guasch, J. Luis & Foster, Vivien (2005), "How Profitable Are Infrastructure Concessions in Latin America? Empirical Evidence and Regulatory Implications", Trends and Policy Options, No. 2, PPI-AF, The World Bank, Washington, DC.

Stern, Jon and Cubbin, John (2005), "Regulatory Effectiveness: The Impact of Regulation and Regulatory Governance Arrangements on Electricity Industry Outcomes", World Bank Policy Research Working Paper # 3536, The World Bank, Washington, DC.

UNDP/World Bank (1999), Global Energy Sector Reform in Developing Countries: A Scorecard, Energy and Mining Sector Unit, The World Bank, Washington, DC.

USAID (1995), Minimum Debt Financing Requirements for Private Power Projects in India, prepared by Hagler Bailly Consulting, Inc., Arlington, VA.

Venketesan, R. & Varma, S. (1998), Policy Competition Among States in India for Attracting Foreign Direct Investment, National Council of Applied Economic Research, New Delhi.

Woo, P. Y. (2005a), Independent Power Producers in Thailand, Working Paper # 51, Program on Energy and Sustainable Development, Center for Environmental Science and Policy, Stanford University, Stanford, CA.

WOO, P. Y. (2005b), "China's Electric Power Market: The Rise and Fall of IPPs", Working Paper # 45, Program on Energy and Sustainable Development, Center for Environmental Science and Policy, Stanford University, Stanford, CA.

WOODHOUSE, Erik J. (2005a), "The Experience of Independent Power Producers in Developing Countries", Final Report, Program on Energy and Sustainable Development, Center for Environmental Science and Policy, Stanford University, Stanford, CA.

WOODHOUSE, Erik J. (2005b), "The IPP Experience in the Philippines", Working Paper #37, Program on Energy and Sustainable Development, Center for Environmental Science and Policy, Stanford University, Stanford, CA.

WB/IFC (2004), "India: Investment Climate and Manufacturing Industry", The World Bank and the International Finance Corporation, Washington, DC.

WORLD BANK (2006), *World Development Indicators 2006*, The World Bank, Washington, DC.

WORLD BANK (2005a), *World Development Report 2005: A Better Investment Climate For Everyone*, The World Bank, Washington, DC.

WORLD BANK (2005b), *Global Development Finance 2005: Mobilizing Finance and Managing Vulnerability*, The World Bank, Washington, DC.

WORLD BANK (2005c), "Infrastructure and the World Bank", A report for the Development Committee Meeting, The World Bank, Washington, DC.

WORLD BANK (2004), The Challenge of Financing Infrastructure in Developing Countries, in *Global Development Finance 2004: Harnessing Cyclical Gains for Development*, The World Bank, Washington, DC.

WORLD BANK (2003), "Implementing the World Bank Group Infrastructure Action Plan (with special emphasis on follow-up to the recommendations of the World Panel on financing water infrastructure)", The World Bank, Washington, DC.

ZHANG, Y., PARKER, D. and KIRKPATRICK, C. (2004), "Competition, Regulation and Privatisation of Electricity Generation in Developing Countries: Does the Sequencing of the Reforms Matter?", Working Paper # 62, The Centre on Regulation and Competition is hosted by the Institute for Development Policy and Management (IDPM), School of Environment and Development (SED), University of Manchester, Manchester.

Appendix A

S.No.	Name of the Projects	CAP (MW) & Date of Commissioning
IPP projects accorded techno-economic clearance (TEC) by CEA		
1	Paguthan CCGT (M/s Gujarat PowerGen Energy Corp.), Gujarat	655 (13.10.98)
2	Hazira CCGT (M/s. Essar Power Ltd.), Gujarat	515 (26.05.97)
3	Baroda CCGT (M/s. GIPCL), Gujarat	167 (18.11.97)
4	Surat Lignite TPP (M/s GIPCL), Gujarat	250 (16.01.2000)
5	Dabhol CCGT (Ph-I) (M/s. Dabhol Power Co.), Maharashtra	740 (May, 99)
6	Jegurupadu CCGT (M/s. GVK Industries), Andhra Pradesh	216.0 (20.06.97)
7	Godavari CCGT (M/s. Specturam Tech.), Andhra Pradesh	206.2 (31.03.98)
8	Basin Bridge DGPP (M/s. GMR Power Corp Pvt Ltd), Tamil Nadu	200 (31.12.98)
9	Torangallu TPS (M/s. Jindal Tractebel), Karnataka	260 (16.5.99)
10	Kondapally CCGT (M/s Kondapally Power Corp Ltd.), Andhra Pradesh	350 (18.10.2000)
11	Samalpatti DGPP (M/s Samalpatti Power Co.,), T. N.	105.66 (March, 2001)
12	Pillaiperumalnallur CCGT (M/s PPN Power Gen. Comp.), T. N.	330.5 (04.04.2001)
13	Malana HEP (Solano Power Company Ltd.) (H. P.), H. P.	86 (July, 2001)
14	Samayanallur DGPP (M/s Madurai Power Corp. Pvt. Ltd.) T. N.	106 (22.09.01)
15	Jojobera TPS (M/s Jamshedpur Power Co. Ltd.), Jharkhand	240 (October, 2000)
16	Neyveli lignite TPP of M/s ST- CMS Electric Co., TN	250 (11.10.02)
17	Baspa HEP (3 x 100 MW), Himachal Pradesh (Ms. Jaiprakash Hydro Power Ltd.)	300 (27.05.03)
	Sub-Total A	**5977.36**
IPP projects which do not require TEC of CEA		
18	Guntur Branch Canal-I HEP, Andhra Pradesh	3.75 (1996-1997)
19	Shivpur HEP (M/s Bhoruka Power Company), Karnataka	18 (1992-1993)
20	Maniyar HEP (Carborandum Universal), Kerala	12 (1994-1995)

21	Reliance Salgaocar Project, Goa	48 (1999-2000)
22	Adamtilla GBPP (M/s DLF Power Co. Ltd.), Assam	9 (1997-1998)
23	Bansakandi GBPP (M/s DLF Power Co. Ltd.), Assam	15.5 (1997-1998)
24	Gurgaon CCGT (M/s Magnum Power), Haryana	25 (1999-2000)
25	Tawa HEP (M/s Hindustan Electro Graphite), Madhya Pradesh	13.5 (1996-1997)
26	B5E5(Kerala)Eloor Project (M/s BSES (Kerala) Ltd), Kerala	173 (1999-2000)
27	Belgaum DGPP (M/s Tata Power Co. Ltd), Karnataka	81.3
28	Tanir Bavi Barge Mounted Power Plant (Tanir Bavi Power Co.), Karnataka	220 (8.6.01- Simple Cycle) 21.11.2001 (Combined Cycle)
29	Peddapuram CCGT (M/s. Reliance Energy Ltd) A. P	78 (2002)
30	LVS Power Ltd., Andhra Pradesh	36.8 (October, 2001)
31	Bellary Power Project (AA/s. Rayalseema Alkalies & Allied Chemicals Ltd.), Karnataka	27.8 (Sep., 2000)
32	Bambooflat DGPP (AA/s Surya-chakra Power Corp. Ltd.) A&N Islands	20 (2002-2003)
33	Karuppur (Tanjore) CCPP (Aban Power Co. Ltd.) (Gas)	113.2 (11.08.05)
34	Jegurupadu Exp (Gas) M/s. GVK Industries Ltd.	80 (11.11.05)
	Sub total B	**974.85**
Private power projects set up by licensee companies		
35	New Southern Gen. Station (M/s CESC Ltd), Calcutta	135 (1992-1993)
36	Trombay TPP (M/s BSES), Maharashtra	180 (1993-1994) (1994-1995)
37	Dahanu TPP (M/s BSES), Maharashtra	500 (1994-1995)
38	Bhira PSS (M/s Tata Electric Com.), Maharashtra	150 (1995-1996)
39	Budge-Budge TPP (M/s CESC), W. Bengal	500 (1997-1998)
	Sub total C	**1465**
Grand Total A+B+C		**7417.21**

Source: Ministry of Power

Appendix B

	X Plan			XI Plan			
Description	State	Central	Private	State	Central	Private	Total
Funds required	177000	178000	45000	219000	195000	86000	900000
(A) Equity Required	**53100**	**53400**	**13500**	**65700**	**58500**	**25800**	**270000**
(B) Equity Available							
1. Promoters incl. FDI	0	0	5000	0	0	9500	14500
2. Internal Resources	5000	19000	1000	20000	18000	2000	65000
3. Govt Support							
3.1 State Govt.	10000	0	0	10000	0	0	20000
3.2 Central Govt.	# 10000	28000	0	10000	38000	0	86000
3.3 PMGY /Kutir Jyoti Grants	6000	0		9000			15000
(C) Total (B)	**31000**	**47000**	**6000**	**49000**	**56000**	**11500**	**200500**
(D) Equity Gap (A-C)	**22100**	**6400**	**7500**	**16700**	**2500**	**14300**	**69500**
(E) Debt Required	**123900**	**124600**	**31500**	**153300**	**136500**	**60200**	**630000**
(F) Debt Available							
1. Domestic							
1.1 Direct market borrowing	6000	8600	6000	15000	10000	7000	52600
1.2 Banks and AIFIs	40900	90000	13100	29300	78500	18200	270000
1.3 PFC	20000	9000	5400	45000	27000	20000	126400
1.4 REC	32000	0	0	36000	4000	8000	80000
1.5 Central Govt.	# 10000	0	0	10000	0	0	20000
2. International							
2.1 Multilateral/ bilateral credits	10000	5000	0	10000	5000	0	30000

2.2 ECA/ECB/Syn. loan etc.	5000	12000	7000	8000	12000	7000	51000
(G) Total (F)	**123900**	**124600**	**31500**	**153300**	**136500**	**60200**	**630000**
(H) Debt Gap (E-G)	**0**	**0**	**0**	**0**	**0**	**0**	
(I) Total Gap (D+H)	**22100**	**6400**	**7500**	**16700**	**2500**	**14300**	**69500**

Source: GOI (2002a)
Note: # - APDRP Funding

About the Author

Dr. Anoop Singh holds a PhD in the area of energy economics from Indira Gandhi Institute of Development Research, Mumbai. He is also a graduate in Mechanical Engg. and a post graduate in Industrial Engineering. He is currently an Associate Professor at the Dept. of Industrial and Management Engineering, Indian Institute of Technology Kanpur. Before joining IIT Kanpur in 2001, he worked with the Indian Council for Research on International Economic Relations, New Delhi and the Haryana Electricity Regulatory Commission, Panchkula.

His areas of interest include infrastructure regulation, policy and finance, power market reform and regulation, energy efficiency, renewable energy, energy and environment, project financing, energy economics and cross-border energy cooperation.

He has undertaken a number of research/consultancy projects related to electricity/energy sector for a number of institutions including the World Bank, the UNCTAD, UNU/IAS, AIT, the University of Cambridge, and the Planning Commission. He has also contributed a number of regulatory and policy submissions with reference to formulation of regulations and policies. He has a number of conference, discussion and journal papers to his credit. He was also the Guest Editor to the International Journal of Energy Sector Management (special issue related to India). He is a Senior Member of IEEE, a member of International Association for Energy Economics (IAEE) and Life Member of Indian Economic Association (IEA).

He was Member of the Working Group on Power for the 11th Five-Year Plan, Planning Commission, Government of India. He was also a member of the Core Group on Next Generation Networks (Licensing Issues), Telecom Regulatory Authority of India (TRAI) and Member, Electricity Contract Advisory Board of Multi Commodity Exchange of India (MCX), Mumbai. He is currently Member, Advisory Committee for Capacity Building of Distribution Personnel under R-APDRP, Ministry of Power and also a Member of the Research Advisory Committee of Council of Power Utilities, New Delhi.

Made in the USA
Las Vegas, NV
03 November 2026

57422194R00081